Empowering Young Leaders

The ethos, culture, and climate of a school lie at the very heart of its success and have a dramatic impact on the future of its students. This exciting new book shows how through values-based, inclusive, and aspirational leadership, teachers and school leaders can support students in becoming well rounded, globally minded change-makers of the future. Based on the principle that every young person can be a leader, it offers step-by-step guidance to support the development of leadership skills and shows how leadership opportunities can be made accessible to all learners.

Arguing that leadership needs to be actively and inclusively taught, the book explores how young leadership models, reward systems, risk-taking, well-being strategies, and growth-mindset implementation can transform student motivation levels by creating aspiration, fulfilling dreams, and building character. Packed with practical suggestions and resources, the chapters cover:

- diversity and leadership

- establishing a strong student leadership team

- how to meaningfully mark significant global days

- making the most of tutor time

- student well-being

- fear of failure and how to overcome this

- building links with the local and wider community.

Written by a Director of Ethos at an outstanding Trust, this is essential reading for all teachers and school leaders wanting their students to become empathetic, ambitious, values-driven, and happy young people.

Gohar Khan is Director of Ethos & Culture at the Ridgeway Education Trust. Her research interests have included Post-Colonial and Feminist Literature, and more recently, Gohar has devoted herself to exploring, enriching, and expanding school ethos, culture, and the possibilities that come from investing in values-based student leadership. Gohar has 15 years of experience as a teacher and school leader and has worked with several schools to establish their own ethos and young leadership programmes worldwide.

I have been lucky enough to personally witness the inspirational work of Dr Gohar Khan. This book is essential for any leader who is serious about developing a forward looking and rich school culture which encourages all students to develop as leaders. The book combines strategic insight with very practical tips which will support school leaders in developing youngsters who are articulate, resilient, courageous, curious and have the confidence to stand up for what they believe in. Get this book!

Manny Botwe, ASCL Vice President

Empowering Young Leaders

How your Culture and Ethos can Enhance Student Leadership within your School

Gohar Khan

Routledge
Taylor & Francis Group

LONDON AND NEW YORK

Designed cover image: © Getty Images

First published 2024
by Routledge
4 Park Square, Milton Park, Abingdon, Oxon OX14 4RN

and by Routledge
605 Third Avenue, New York, NY 10158

Routledge is an imprint of the Taylor & Francis Group, an informa business

© 2024 Gohar Khan

The right of Gohar Khan to be identified as author of this work has been asserted in accordance with sections 77 and 78 of the Copyright, Designs and Patents Act 1988.

British Library Cataloguing-in-Publication Data
A catalogue record for this book is available from the British Library

ISBN: 978-1-032-23152-5 (hbk)
ISBN: 978-1-032-23150-1 (pbk)
ISBN: 978-1-003-27598-5 (ebk)

DOI: 10.4324/9781003275985

Typeset in Melior
by codeMantra

For my students, who fill me with purpose and pride

Contents

Acknowledgements

When you start out writing a book, I am not sure you entirely believe it will turn into a book. I know I didn't. My dream to write about young leaders and change makers has become a reality owing to the encouragement, support, cheering on and contributions of several wonderful people:

Rachael Warwick, CEO of the Ridgeway Education Trust, who is the most visionary leader I have ever known and who made me realise just how much culture matters. My thanks go to Rachael for being my mentor and a champion on my work in the Trust, always.

George Littler and Will Manning, Headteachers at Didcot Girls' School and St. Birinus School respectively, for leading the two most inspirational teams I have ever worked with. I thank them for their guidance, their wisdom, and their dedication to all things Ethos.

Rachel Hornsey and Lisa Knight, Headteacher and Assistant Headteacher at Sutton Courtenay Primary School have my deep gratitude for their vision, time and generosity in sharing ideas and resources. I learn from them and their wonderful team all the time.

Paul Comina, my Ethos 'partner in crime' for the huge amount of work he does to cultivate young leadership and remains humble through it all. Paul is so devoted to this good work, and never seeks any credit for his efforts. Thank you to Paul for keeping me grounded and for his friendship.

Stuart George, an Award-winning Careers specialist at the Trust, who is my sounding board and advisor and whose work aligns so closely with Ethos. I am grateful to Stuart for spending time talking to me about Careers and Personal Development and for making this book all the better for it.

Sandra Cohen, our Head of German and all-round fascinating colleague who has mastery over many languages and a vision for all her students to gain the best experiences they can. Huge thanks to Sandra for sharing her time and thoughts so generously with me.

Stella Vassiliou, firstly, for being the absolute epitome of brilliant teaching, and secondly for her determination to help young people find and use their voices. Everyone ultimately just wants to be taught by 'Miss V'.

Harriet Edwards, for the inspiration and direction she provided in organising our House Shout.

Cat Marshall, Fern Goldsmith, Charlie Osborne and Beth Coombes for their dedication to Rainbow Club and Community Club and their passion for inclusivity. Phil Mahoney, Liam Purnell and Naomi Sharland for their commitment to all things Ethos and wider-school life. Adam Tamplin for the immense amount of work he does to make tutor time so powerful for all students and for being an excellent colleague to work with.

Rachel Beard, Karen Grain, and Rebecca Porter, without whose help the Leadership Ladder could not run as beautifully as it does.

My incredible colleagues across the Ridgeway Education Trust who never fail to remind me why we teachers do the most important job in the world! I want to give a special mention to Team English, also popularly known as Team Gold, for being the best colleagues anyone can dream of having. The front cover of the book was inspired by our outgoing Head of English and my friend, Lara Martin.

My student leaders, who are the reason I do what I do, and without whose support and warmth Ethos would just not exist in the way it does at the Trust. I am grateful for their good humour, teamwork, enthusiasm, and leadership. In particular, I wish to thank Chloe Cormack (Head Student) and Sydnie Dougan (House Captain) for making time to contribute to this book. They are just exceptional!

I am so grateful to the team at Routledge for their patience with me while I built this manuscript, word by word. Thank you!

Without the support of our childminders, Kate Adam, and Anna Hadland, I would just not have the time or energy to put pen to paper. I hope they know how grateful I am!.

My incredible friends Sana Balagamwala and Vedita Cowalusoor, both wonderful writers, have been cheering me on right from the start – I would be rather lost without their friendship and encouragement. My life-long friends Shafia, Saadia, Sobia and Sehr who have had such a deep influence on my own values and identity – thank you.

I want to thank my PhD supervisor, Dr Pablo Mukherjee, who made me throw so many chapters out of the window that he actually made a decent writer of me! I also wish to thank all my teachers, who is some way, shape or form have influenced my thinking and learning.

Ian Wigston for believing in my work and for supporting me with the publishing process.

My sister Saba, a novelist, filmmaker, confidant, and lifetime supporter of all my ventures. Saba has inspired me and given me the confidence to dream to be a writer. Saba's family for making us all laugh and smile though the process.

My brother Farrukh, for being honest, solid and annoyingly clever; for not letting anything get past him. Farrukh's family for being wonderfully supportive and loving.

My mother, who has said to me since I was very young, 'You have a book in you. Write it'; for her love, encouragement and persistence in all situations. She may not know this, but she is an outstanding advocate for the Growth Mindset theory!

My husband Omar, well known for his brutal honesty, and without whose advice to 'just write and hand it in', I would probably still be making notes. I am grateful to Omar for being by my side, no matter what, always. I am also grateful to my husband's parents who have always prayed for my success.

My daughter Aleena for believing in me and for laughing at all my jokes, even the truly dreadful ones. I often forget I am her parent and not her friend; she is wiser than many adults and has inspired so much of my thinking about young leadership. I hope she has many successes as a wonderful public speaker.

My son Samih, who is wise and creative and extraordinary; his insights are always mind-blowing, and I know he has a book in him too one day! I hope that one day he will realise just how incredible his mind is and do something marvellous with it.

My youngest one, Razi, whose arrival prompted me to want to do something other than feeding and changing nappies for a year. I am grateful for the smiles and laughter he has brought into our house. Razi is the light in our lives and the reason we never stop cleaning the floors.

My late father, Rafat Karim, who taught me to love words – to read and to write – and to understand that education is everything. I am grateful to him for teaching me to approach life and people with compassion, no matter what.

If I have missed anyone out, I am genuinely very sorry. Blame an under slept mother of an unstoppable toddler. You have my thanks all the same.

Foreword

It's easy to write history backwards. Putting Ethos at the heart of school improvement when appointed as a first-time Headteacher of a school that had great potential but had hit tough times proved to be a lucky 'best bet'. This is going back nearly 15 years and, at this time, there was no well-documented evidence base that led to this decision. It was pure instinct. I knew that I could build a good school through high-quality implementation of behaviour systems and a well-planned curriculum taught by well-trained and motivated staff, but I wanted my students to experience an exceptional education. What would this look like? More than excellent teaching and learning. More than impeccable behaviour. More than excellent results....

In my first week in post, I received an email from Stanley, a boy I had taught at my previous school, a wonderful young person with huge potential. He wrote: *"I am writing under the assumption you have forgotten me by now, but I felt it important to email you because you've been an incredible inspiration since you taught me GCSE English. Although at the time I didn't fully appreciate it, you taught me to believe in myself and that hard work and ambition could mean achieving things I thought were for the select few. I have now decided to study a joint degree between UCL and LSE in engineering and economics and am in the process of starting a venture capital firm in Tanzania. I am very optimistic about the future. I wish you success in your new role and hope you continue to inspire more pupils to be the best they can be".*

I learnt two things from Stan's message. Firstly, to set up a folder for any lovely emails I received that I could read again on days when I received not-so lovely emails, days when courage or inspiration were in short supply. Secondly, if I did have the potential to inspire young people to believe in themselves, to aim high, and realise their huge potential, then this was the ethos I wanted for my own school and for all our students.

I wanted all our young people to enjoy coming to school every day, to feel part of a community, to feel pride in their school, and to leave us with happy memories and a strong sense of agency, as well as great qualifications. I knew that everything good in a school could only be achieved through a team effort, through the leadership and role modelling of adults who felt that they were appreciated and had their own strong sense of agency. I knew we were on the right path when a few years into my headship, I received another lovely email from a member of staff entitled: 'Cultural Change at DGS'. It read: "*I wanted to email you because I have been in the blessed position of receiving lots of positive feedback in a range of ways, from a range of sources over the last couple of weeks, and I really wanted to say thank you. You have created a culture in our school where people are happy to celebrate the good things that they see, to pass on things that have inspired them, and to share positive experiences. As a result of that culture, I have enjoyed wonderful, heart-warming communication with colleagues, with parents and with students, which have made me not only proud, but genuinely happy to work in a school where people say thank you*".

Building a strong culture, a clear sense of "how we do things here", has to be based on values that are owned by the school community and expressed in practical, everyday ways. This was our first step. Creating a rich offer of student leadership opportunities and finding ways to reward and celebrate young people for their engagement was a relatively easy win. Unsurprisingly, the ethos was created largely through listening to and working with young people. (It still surprises me that some school leaders feel that they can dictate values to young people and prescribe an ethos to their staff.) We used whole school assemblies to showcase the school's ethos of ambition and agency: students performed and presented to and celebrated one another and the staff, including myself, took a back seat. A virtuous cycle emerged where relationships between staff and students and students and students thrived and this, in turn, led to discretionary effort which created more opportunities for young people and more engagement with them. This sense of agency and ownership nurtured a creative excitement which made (most) conversations with staff and students an absolute joy.

Change and innovation is so important to sustain growth, and this is true for schools too. When Dr Gohar Khan walked through my door to interview for an English teacher post in 20xx, I instinctively felt I had met the change the school needed. Over time, Gohar took over the role of Head of Ethos for Didcot Girls' School and then Director of Ethos for our Trust. Gohar embodies our Trust values and our Trust Ethos. She has brought fresh thinking, navigating thoughtfully and with real credibility the complex landscape of the global shifts we have all lived through over the last few years. Gohar brought with her an international perspective that has hugely benefited our schools. She has moved our definition of Ethos on to include an ongoing discussion of international events and to embrace our equality, diversity, and inclusion strategy. She has placed student well-being firmly at the heart of the Ethos agenda. Student leadership roles have now expanded to include Diversity Leaders, Climate Leaders, and Community Leaders. An exceptional careers provision has been neatly woven into the student leadership programme. What hasn't changed is the focus on all children, especially those who are disadvantaged, being at the heart of our Ethos work.

I have learnt so much from working with Gohar. The mantra that the best leaders actively seek out people with domain expertise which surpasses their own is one I have found to be true again and again, not least in Gohar. (Or at least I take comfort in this mantra to think that I am not yet completely superfluous to requirements!). I recommend Gohar's book to you wholeheartedly. You will find it a treasure trove of practical and accessible ways to simply make your school or college better. Of course, everything is context specific, but there is much in this book which is transferrable and can easily be adapted to suit your particular context. The ethos at Didcot Girls' School is based on girls becoming future leaders and change-makers, of breaking the glass ceilings which still exist for women in society. St Birinus School, the boys' school in our Trust, has shaped its ethos around modern masculinity, an empowering and much-needed narrative for boys and young men.

Our primary school, Sutton Courtenay CofE Primary School, has created an ethos around children developing their voice, realising their agency to make positive change in the world.

As ASCL (Association of School and College Leaders) President 2019–2020, I chose my theme for the year as 'Diversity in Leadership'. I used my position to hold a mirror up to the lack of diversity in ASCL itself, as well as in the leadership of our schools and colleges up and down the country, and to drive positive change. We know that young people cannot be what they cannot see. Change is slow. There is still so much work to be done. It is books like this which help to change the world, page by page. I am extremely grateful to Gohar for writing it and for all she has done, and continues to do, for our children and young people. She is helping to build a legacy of which we can all be extremely proud.

Rachael Warwick
CEO and Executive Headteacher
Ridgeway Education Trust
March 2023

Introduction

First things first: I use the term 'Ethos' a great deal in this book. In the interest of ease as you read on, I want to clarify the parameters and scope of the term at the outset. When I talk about ethos, I am referring to school culture in the widest sense of the phrase, but I am also traversing values, enrichment, wider school life, well-being, growth mindset, global awareness, oracy, and my personal favourite, young leadership. Ethos is a remarkably wonderful term in that it allows us to capture the way the school 'feels', which is at once instinctive and complex. Very much in line with the Aristotelian meaning of the term, the ethos of a school is its moral character; it's what makes our schools credible and worthy of trust. Second, my experiences, evidence, and examples all come from my work at The Ridgeway Education Trust, based in South Oxfordshire. The Trust comprises an all-girls' state secondary and all-boys' state secondary and a mixed state primary school currently, but even as I write, we are growing in size. In terms of student numbers, at the time of writing, this growing Trust is made up of circa 2,500 students in total. Finally, all the chapters in this book offer a combination of thoughts, suggestions, case studies, and conversations with some of the best people I have come across in the world of education – or indeed in the world! I am grateful for the insights of my colleagues and for their generosity in sharing their time and thoughts so willingly with me. Each chapter starts with a signpost of what to expect and ends with a 'Tool Kit' which captures the salient features of the chapter, particularly action points, some of which may be implementable straight away. Thank you for picking up this book; I truly hope the pages that follow will offer some food for thought.

The ethos, culture, and climate of a school lie at the very heart of its success. Investing in these will reap phenomenal rewards, and yet, in many educational institutions, ethos is viewed as a luxury: business class travel where economy will suffice. Not for a moment would I suggest this anyone's 'fault' – the reality is that state sector schools are in a crisis and are facing tough challenges, including recruitment, an unprecedented rise in mental health problems, staff shortage, and an appalling lack of funds. These problems are real and demand our immediate attention. Ethos and culture, however, must not be held in abeyance pending solutions to these problems. Ironically, making time for culture to thrive can be a crucial part of the solution, and this book shows you why and how this happens. When we remain in a constant state of fight and flight, the blue-sky and the bigger picture becomes hazy and distant; in this mode, we are mainly out to ensure that the day or the week or the term is completed without serious disruption, before we take a breath and ready ourselves for the next stretch. I want to show you that stopping for a moment, reflecting on school ethos and culture, values, and vision, can ground us as a school community as we continue to respond to the challenges facing us. It can significantly enhance our well-being and dial up our levels of motivation. It can bring back the joy and reignite the spark of ambition that young people seem to have lost a little, especially after months of unprecedented Covid-19 lockdowns. Creating, recreating, or doing a wholesale revamp of the ethos provision at your school may not be the magic potion that we could all do with in the world of education, but it is an incredibly powerful part of the process of making schools a place where young people want to be. Ethos matters. Culture matters. Working to get this right will make a tremendous difference to entire school communities. That is the good news.

The less good news is that it is entirely facile to hope that a rich and thriving ethos will be a handy by-product of everything else that happens in schools. Ethos needs to be cultivated and nurtured. Leadership needs to be taught to young people – actively and inclusively. Enrichment requires judicious planning; cultural capital needs to be reinforced by continual research. Only then can we hope to create the next generation of visionary leaders, innovators, and change-makers – a job we cannot afford to mismanage. This can feel understandably daunting, as we can find ourselves asking, "how does one create a culture"? Culture is something you expect to inherit or glide into, without necessarily even perceiving it. It is generally either when things are going rather well or very poorly in your professional environment that you think to blame this nebulous concept we call culture. So yes, cultural shifts are difficult to initiate. I suggest that a rich and diverse provision for young leadership is a good place for schools to start.

Leadership at any level has traditionally been viewed as the preserve of the few: an exclusive position which most individuals find either daunting or entirely irrelevant. With the support of brilliant colleagues and the vision created by our CEO, Rachael Warwick, I have spent the past eight years at *The Ridgeway Education Trust* complicating and reimagining traditional tropes of student leadership and working to create a culture where leadership is inclusive, accessible, exciting, and purposeful. Any educator will testify to the joy felt when encountering a happy, successful, and confident individual whom they once had the privilege of teaching. It is the ultimate validation of our daily work. The futures of our students are paramount to us, and it is my belief that creating, feeding, and sustaining a culture of ambition, leadership, and well-being is the best way to prepare our young people to become the change-makers of the future.

Our young people have a great deal to look forward to in their futures, but there are undeniable challenges: political uncertainty, unprecedented digitalisation, an unknown job culture, the crisis concerning climate change, and most recently, a new world order created by Covid-19. Considering this context, how can we best prepare our students to dare to dream? This book, based on several years of experience and the organic growth of the Trust I work for, is packed with ideas for the cultivation of a powerful school ethos with values-based student leadership at its heart. It explores the correlation between a strong, thriving ethos and consistent academic success. Moreover, it confirms the causal link between ethos, values, and student well-being.

The Trust I work at currently comprises three schools: an all-girls' secondary of circa 1,500 students, an all-boys' secondary of circa 1,000 students, and a primary school comprising just under 250 pupils. Our Ethos at both secondary schools is driven by the aim to nurture the next generation of leaders and change-makers who recognise the power of values-based leadership: resilience, compassion, ambition, empathy, global awareness, and the will to make a difference. The ambition to challenge misconceptions young men and masculinity and develop an awareness of modern masculinity is at the centre of our Ethos provision at the boys' school, and we strongly believe in the positive impact this experience will have on the futures of our students. At the girls' school, we have the additional focus of equipping our young women with the knowledge that compassion and courage can coexist and that all opportunities, barring none, are available to them. At the primary school, the ethos is vibrant and rich: children begin to make their first forays into what leadership can feel like, how empowering it can be to speak in public and understand empathy by learning about the world in a variety of ways. Our work in the Trust is truly a journey, and there are several hopes and aspirations yet to be realised. We are however incredibly proud of the ethos we have created and are excited to share this more widely (Figures 0.1–0.4).

The book offers a comprehensive step-by-step approach on how to imagine, create, and embed a powerful ethos provision in any school or college, irrespective of performance data. It delves into young leadership models, reward systems, risk-taking, well-being strategies, growth-mindset implementation, and a rich ethos calendar. School leaders will benefit from detailed information on how to meaningfully mark significant global days, including International Day of the Girl, International Women's Day, International Men's Day, Anti-Bullying Week, Black History Month, Pride Month, and Holocaust Memorial Day to name a few. Additionally, templates and resources will be provided for our nationally recognised annual Student Leadership Conference. My hope is that this book will be the one-stop resource for educational institutions wishing to integrate outstanding culture, ethos, and leadership into their journey.

My official title at the Trust is 'Director of Ethos'. Despite their best efforts to disguise it, the slightly perplexed look on people's faces when I tell them this, is unmistakable. What does a Director of Ethos do? To the best of my limited knowledge, there are no other Directors of Ethos in the UK, hence the looks of

Figure 0.1 Primary school children in the Ridgeway Education Trust.

Figure 0.2 Remembrance day photograph.

Figure 0.3 Footballers at Didcot Girls' School.

Figure 0.4 Students winning medals.

bemusement. The beauty of this role, and the growing Ethos team that accompanies it, is that there is someone who gets time and a salary to keep asking the following crucial questions:

- Is our climate and culture conducive to curiosity?
- Do we have diverse, eclectic, and purposeful structures for young leadership?
- What provisions do we have in place for leadership at primary and sixth form levels?
- Do you deliberately do enough to create joy in our community?
- Are we listening to what students have to say all the time?
- Do our students understand the school values, live by them, and use them to start thinking about their own set of values?
- Are we doing enough to help young people understand what is unfolding in the world around them?
- How much do our students contribute to our local community and how can we help them do more?
- Do our disadvantaged students have equal and excellent access to our wider school life and enrichment offer?
- Does our House system create a strong sense of community and healthy competition?
- Are we inclusive of *all* our students when it comes to young leadership?
- How rich and diverse is our Ethos calendar and where are the gaps?
- Are our students equipped with the tools of emotional literacy they need to communicate with us and others around them?
- Are we just talking about 'Growth Mindset' a lot, or implementing it meaningfully?
- What are we doing to contribute to countering the impact of climate change? Is it enough?
- How are we approaching growing anxiety within young people?
- Assemblies are gold dust: are we using these wisely?

If you find that any of the above questions strike a chord with you, read on. This book has been written with the absolute confidence that we all want to do what is right and best by our young people. I hope the following chapters offer some insights that prove useful on your own journey as a school, or at the very least, pique your curiosity (Figures 0.5–0.8).

Figure 0.5 Culture evening.

Figure 0.6 Students celebrate Diwali at School.

Figure 0.7 Boys in briefing.

Figure 0.8 School picnic.

Debunking leadership myths

Read on to: explore and dismantle the most common and damaging myths about leadership and find tangible and practical advice on how to help young people form a better, more wholesome relationship with leadership.

"Mastering others is strength. Mastering yourself is true power."

– Lao Tzu

Countering the urge to be invisible

I have lost count of the number of times I have been approached by young people across the schools I have taught in, sheepishly confessing their lack of interest in our student leadership programmes, on the pretext that "I am not a natural leader Miss"; "Leadership isn't for me to be honest"; and "I don't plan to become a leader in the future" etcetera. It is so much easier to be invisible rather than visible. In my secondary school life, I frequently sought opportunities to disappear from the radar for wider school life because this way I could completely avoid all the emotional investment that I assumed would come with public-facing role. I could avoid sleepless nights before speaking in assembly, conversations with the senior leadership team, liaising with older year groups, or drawing attention to myself in any way that was more than strictly necessary. My father believed with all his heart that when opportunities were presented to us at school, we had a responsibility to, at the very least, *try* to avail them. In particular, he encouraged me to audition for any public speaking opportunities that arose. He explained that this was something of a family tradition: my great-grandfather was a debater, my grandfather made speeches all over the world, my father was a professor and so public speaking came naturally to him. So, the baton was passed down to me, who, reluctantly, began to appear at auditions for debate teams, elocutions, and oracy competitions. It was nerve wrecking – and not in a way that felt normal or wholesome. (Afterall, some nerves are meant to boost our public speaking performance.) I was terrified to a point where my sleep and appetite were affected, and I derived no enjoyment from the process at all. When I saw my peers who seemed to embrace these opportunities much more naturally and confidently, my ego took a further bruising: not only was I pathetically nervous and anxious about leadership, but others around me were also basking in the excitement of it all. Well, that's the narrative I told myself in any case. By the end of secondary school, so deep was my inner conflict about being a talented public speaker my father could be proud of and wishing never to climb the stairs to a stage again, that I decided to keep away from any sort of leadership opportunity once I left school. Life's little ironies are a lovely thing and here I am doing everything in my power to promote leadership skills in young people, often addressing thousands of students at a time to do so. What's changed? In the main, my understanding of leadership and leaders and a heightened awareness of the myths that have historically surrounded leadership.

Changing a mindset

When I began my work on ethos at the Ridgeway Education Trust, I knew that my first mission was to debunk the myths surrounding leadership and dismantle common misconceptions that leave young people indifferent to – and sometimes downright petrified of – the idea of leading. I distinctly remember my very first assembly on this subject to 1,200 students and 150 staff, with approximately 16 minutes to convince them that leadership was the rightful concern of each and every individual in that hall; that all of them had a future to shape, visions to set, and ambitions to fulfil. They had a set of values to determine and align with, values which would steer and guide them through the trajectory of their lives; career paths to choose – careers that would bring them purpose, satisfaction, and joy; decisions to make about life, love, and relationships; children to raise, quite possibly; the environmental crisis and climate change to consider; their physical and mental well-being to look after and the world of unprecedented digitalisation to grasp. They had a responsibility to grow and thrive in a world that can sometimes feel ambiguous, complex, and in light of recent events (I am writing at a time when the Covid-19 pandemic is far from over and the world waits and watches as Ukraine, an independent and democratic nation, faces invasion) bizarre. I explained to them what Andree Bryant calls the "inner game" and the importance of doing the work on mindset before embarking on the "outer game" or the action (Author: Andrew Bryant and Ana Lucia Kazan, 2012). I beckoned the ancient Greeks and conveyed the significance of "know thy self"; importantly though, it is not just enough to "know thy self" as in an ever-developing world we also need skills of adaptability and creative problem solving. We will need to lead in times of calm but also in times of crisis. In short, I invited them to dream. The world needs more dreamers, I told them.

Once I had reached the end of this passionate outpouring and paused long enough to ensure it had been absorbed, I asked:

"Who is that one person you will always be responsible for leading?"

This is the question I continue to ask any young person who approaches me to express their lack of interest in leadership. It goes without saying, the answer is always 'Myself' and everyone knows it is impossible to make yourself irrelevant. Once we delineate to our students just how integral leadership is to their life journey, we are beginning to debunk the myth that leadership is elitist, exclusive, unachievable, or irrelevant. Far from being the preserve of the few, it is a way of life that every young person deserves access and exposure to. As educators, once we have done enough to build a solid foundation of values-based leadership, we place our students in the best possible position to lead themselves and ultimately others: to know their own minds well before they start influencing others.

Bryant and Kazan (2012) explore the idea of self-leadership and describe individuals with this quality as having a truly developed sense of who they are, what their capabilities are, and a sense of where they are headed. They define it as "the ability to influence yourself to think and behave in ways that are consistent with who you are and conducive to the pursuit of goals and experiences that are important and relevant to you". I particularly love the idea of "focussing on the one person whom you really can change in life – you – and by doing so becoming someone who can influence others". Bryant and Kazan also reflect on self-leadership as a "journey", which can begin "regardless of where you are in life" – I remind my students that they needn't have a title, role, position, or badge to begin this incredibly fulfilling journey (Autor: Andrew Bryant and Ana Lucia Kazan, 2012). They can start straight away by making a small positive change, followed by a series of small positive changes, alongside taking responsibility for their actions, and understanding that setbacks are a vital part of any journey. Setbacks, I suggest later in the book, are not just inevitable but also invaluable in our growth. Leadership really is that simple when you commit to leading yourself. One small tweak at a time; one little move in the right direction; one nod of appreciation for yourself and your actions. When students truly understand this, leadership feels like an entitlement to them. They perceive it as an opportunity they can't possibly pass up.

Myth 1: leaders always lead a team

They don't. Leaders often set a vision for themselves, as 'unrealistic' as they wish, and set about to realise this vision in a determined and purposeful way. It is entirely possible and quite common for leaders to have just one person on their team: themselves. This message is an important one to deliver to our young people, who are likely to be familiar with traditional tropes of leadership whereby you either lead a team of people or you are a 'follower'. Leading a team that comprises just yourself comes with its own challenges: you take risks and have no one else to blame if they don't pay off and if you feel like a failure, you can't take comfort in a shared experience with others. However, the rewards of self-leadership, when done consciously, can be truly phenomenal. Each little achievement is of your own making and you have been part of the journey every step and stumble of the way. One of the great pleasures of my role at the Trust is the experience of meeting some truly extraordinary leaders, including people who have overcome tremendous self-doubt and fears to keep on their journeys. These are individuals who committed to leading themselves through journeys they felt were important to them; when faced with setbacks, their skills in self-leadership enabled them to recognise that the journey was more important than the obstacles. In this book, I 'showcase' some of these remarkable (they refer to themselves as ordinary, which too is inspiring) individuals. Sarah Outen is an adventurer, speaker, and author of *Dare to Do – Taking on the Planet by Bike and Boat* – she is also well known to me as a warm and compassionate neighbour, which proffers me a great vantage point into her life as an incredible leader and an 'ordinary' human being (Outen, 2018). This is how her website describes Sarah's journey:

> On 1 April 2011, Sarah Outen set off in her kayak from Tower Bridge for France. Her aim was simple: to circle the globe entirely under her own steam – cycling, kayaking and rowing across Europe, Asia, the Pacific, North America, the Atlantic and eventually home. A year later, Sarah was plucked from the Pacific ocean amid tropical storm Mawar, her boat broken, her spirit even more so. But that wasn't the end. Despite ill health and depression, giving up was not an option. So Sarah set off once more to finish what she had started, becoming the first woman to row solo from Japan to Alaska, as well as the first woman to row the mid-Pacific from West to East. She kayaked the treacherous Aleutian chain and cycled North America, before setting out on the Atlantic, despite the risk of another row-ending storm…Dare to Do is more than an adventure story. It is a story of the kindness of strangers and the spirit of travel; a story of the raw power of nature, of finding love in unexpected places, and of discovering your inner strength. It is about trying and failing, and trying again, and about how, even when all seems lost, you can find yourself.
>
> (Outen, n.d.)

Sarah's journey leaves you emotional, awe-struck, moved, and inspired. We are fortunate to have Sarah speak to our students regularly, at events such as our annual Student Leadership Conference on International Women's Day in March. Her's is a story of self-leadership and vulnerability that young people must hear to understand leadership in all its marvellous forms.

Myth 2: you are either a leader or you are not

Let me tell you about Mohammed, who likes to be called Mo, so that is what we will call him in this book. Mo was a shy 15-year old who didn't want anything more from school than just to get through it. The qualities that come to mind when I think of Mo as a student are discipline, a hard work ethic, reflectiveness, and a quiet sensitivity. Mo was friendly yet reserved: he generally kept his head down and looked comfortable enough within his small group of like-minded friends. I often wondered what my assemblies, especially the ones that aimed to inspire and motivate, did for young people like Mo. Did they have to endure my anecdotes and quotations? Did they just ignore my (often loud) enthusiasm at best, or resent it, at worst? I never received any entries to house competitions from Mo. There were no applications to student leadership opportunities, or the desire do anything extra, be it lunchtime clubs or after school activities. When the summer term arrived, and Year 11 and 13 had left after their exams, I decided to devote some time to students such as Mo, who were never regularly found in detention rooms but were also conspicuous by their absence in our wider school life. Talking to Mo, to dig a little deeper, seemed a good place to start. I found a quiet time to speak to him over tutor time, in my office.

ME: "Mo, I am speaking to as many students as I can this week, so this is a completely informal chat. How are you finding things at school the moment?"

MO: "Things are going fine Miss. Everything's good."

ME: "Can you talk to me about three specific things that are going well?"

> After a pause...

MO: "I like Science, PE and DT (Design and Technology)"

ME: "What about outside your timetabled lessons Mo?"

MO: "Some assemblies are okay. I like Sports Day."

> Assemblies! I had something to hang on to now!

ME: "Tell me about the assemblies that have been okay."

> After a much longer pause this time...

MO: "I liked the assembly we had in Anti-Bullying Week last month. It was good to be able to talk to each other. Most assemblies we just have to listen quietly."

> I pressed on as I could sense the possibility of dialogue...

ME: "Tell me more"

MO: "I don't excuse bullying Miss, of course. But in the assembly, you said that sometimes a bystander is no better than a bully. I don't agree with that, but it was interesting to debate it. It made me think that I am often a bystander, but I would never actively bully someone."

The conversation extended longer than anticipated and Mo revealed that he had witnessed acts of bullying on several occasions but had decided against intervening. He explained that calling the bully out felt too confrontational and reporting to a staff member seemed daunting and atypical. I could clearly see the subject had touched a nerve Mo though, and I tentatively asked if he would consider participating in our annual Anti-Bullying Week Roundtable discussion in a few weeks' time. (More on this event to come later in the book.) Mo told me that he would consider this seriously and let me know after the weekend. Whatever came of this conversation, I told myself, I had planted a seed at the very least. Mo did not wait until the weekend to respond to me; instead, I had an email on that same Friday evening.

Please let me know what I need to prepare for the Roundtable Miss. Please may I not have a big speaking part? Have a good weekend.

I smiled, quite literally, from ear to ear. This would be Mo's first foray into young leadership, and I wanted to get it right for him:

Dear Mo,

Thank you very much for getting back to me so promptly. It was a real pleasure to catch you briefly this morning. I am delighted that you will be part of our Anti-Bullying Week Roundtable event. In terms of preparation, please could you consider responses to the following questions:

- *What is bullying? How do you define it?*
- *Everyone deserves to feel safe at school. Does anyone deserve to be bullied?*
- *How do you think other students who are bullied feel?*
- *Bullying is unacceptable. What positive things could you do to be an Upstander if you felt that someone was bullying you? What positive things could you do if you felt that someone else was being bullied?*
- *At what point does conflict between students become bullying?*
- *What can teachers do to help stop bullying?*
- *Have you ever tried to help someone who was being bullied at school? What happened?*
- *What adults do you trust at school to get help with bullying?*
- *Have you or your friends left other kids out on purpose? Do you think that was bullying? Why or why not?*

*I want to assure you that there will be no obligation to speak at any point. We need good speakers **and** good listeners at an event like this. You can expect 19 other students, all from your year group, and there should be a real mix of personalities. Should you wish to, you could bring your ideas on a flashcard and pop it into our suggestions box at the end.*

Hope this helps!
Dr K.

Mo clicked a 'like' on my email, Outlook's recent and most helpful system upgrade. This was enough for me. The next time I saw Mo was at the Roundtable event itself, where he was one of the first to arrive and settle in.

From the perspective of this chapter, where we are dismantling myths about exclusive leadership, it quickly became clear that Mo had a lot to offer and a strong desire to be heard. His peers valued every single one of his contributions and many of these helped to form the basis of longer discussions. In two weeks' time, Mo became a Community Prefect, with lunchtime and breaktime duties on the school premises, responsible for ensuring that pupils felt safe and happy during these times. As a Community Prefect Mo was responsible for being an approachable, friendly figure on the school grounds, who students could approach for help or advice over concerns which he could pass on if needed to a suitable member of staff if needed.

Other than serving as an uplifting anecdote to fellow educators, my working relationship with young people like Mo regularly reminds me that leaders can be grown and nurtured, without any predisposition or divine rights to leadership! I never underestimate the power of a corridor conversation to transform the school experience of a young person.

Mo has since gone on to become a member of the Sixth Form Executive, a body of student leaders responsible for student voice and wider school experiences in Year 12 and 13. Not only has he found his voice, but I would also suggest that he has found himself a little.

Myth 3: to be a good leader, you must be a good speaker...

One aspect of leadership that continues to be a moot point for many young people is public speaking. I have found it very helpful to reassure reluctant leaders about their lack of confidence when it comes to speaking in public, which can feel extremely daunting for the best of leaders! It is misguided to suggest that to be a leader we must also feel confident about addressing large crowds of people. This aspect of leadership can also be worked on and honed over time and is deeply connected to that self-leadership journey which betters over time. We must not forget that there is an important place within leadership for the more quiet, reflective, and sensitive individuals, who, when they do speak, can have quietly powerful impact. I advise making it very clear when appointing student leaders that public speaking is just one aspect of their role and that they can expect plenty of support with. If the prospect of being compelled to speak in an assembly fills a student with terror, and we have done nothing to pre-empt it, we can be fairly sure there will be no applications submitted by them. It is up to us to pre-empt this reluctance to get involved with leadership.

Myth 4: leaders always have impressive 'titles'

The myths surrounding leadership are extensive and far-reaching. Another one I come across in my job is the idea if there is no title, there is no leader. Despite our best efforts to promote young leadership as a Trust, not every single student will have a formal leadership title (or indeed accompanying badge and tie!) It's important that students without such a role can rightly stake a claim to leadership too. This is where leadership opportunities in the classroom can be a game-changer. As part of your pedagogy, consider building in an opportunity for leadership in every lesson. This can range from group leader to whiteboard scribe and decision making to taking on a challenge – just be sure to make the link to leadership clear, so students can benefit from the boost in confidence. I like using a symbol – our yellow leadership lightbulbs indicate to students straight away that there is an opportunity for leadership on offer. And why stop here? If we take leadership as truly values-based, then there is nothing to stop us from being explicit about this connection in lessons too. Creativity, compassion, commitment, care, decision making, listening to others, and showing a positive attitude all count – so why not make them count? In Chapter 2, I go into greater depth about values-based leadership, but for the purpose of this chapter, it is sufficient to recognise that as teachers we are excellently placed to make the links between learning and leadership more explicit, even in the classroom setting.

Myth 5: the leader prototype

There is truly nothing more misleading when it comes to leadership than the notion that leaders are, naturally, extroverts. In my experience, some of the most remarkable leaders are those who work steadily, quietly, and reflectively to realise their visions, as well those of their teams. Jennifer B. Kahnweiler, author of *The Introverted Leader*, does some fascinating research into introverts and their relationship with leadership. According to Kahnweiler, a staggering 40% of executives identify as introverts to whom leadership does not come naturally (Kahnweiler and Conant, 2018). It's empowering for our students to know such statistics and believe that their personalities do not have to come in the way of their leadership journey and may well enhance and expedite it. An example I regularly share with my students is of Warren Buffet, an investment guru, a philanthropist, and the fifth richest man in the world at the time of writing. Buffet is often called an 'introvert' and has frequently talked about how terrified he was of speaking in public when younger. He knew early on that effective communication was an essential skill if he was going to be successful and intentionally put strategies into place to gain confidence in this area. However, even now Buffet seems to be much more comfortable talking reflectively with small groups of people or individuals for prolonged periods of time, given them his full attention and consideration. Karl Moore has written in Forbes about observing Buffet in his interactions with others and reflects:

Firstly, Mr. Buffett spoke easily, comfortably and with very considerable author-ity, but only about things that he knew about – that, as an 87 year old, he had worked on, thought about and studied for decades in most cases. Our research sug-gests that this is very typical of introverted leaders. Extroverts, like myself, are too apt to make it up as we go along; this, of course, can get us into trouble, as it should. Introverts can be just as good communicators as extroverts, but almost always stick to things they know. Mr. Buffett did not pontificate on things that were outside of his expertise, which at his age and experience is a pretty broad set of subjects.

He adds that Buffet appeared unbothered by crowds and instead more than sat-isfied to spend his time having meaningful conversations in smaller groups:

The third and final note was that Warren did his networking as an introvert of-ten does, in small numbers and not worrying about working the crowd as much as an extrovert would. He very graciously took a group picture with each school, but at lunch he sat virtually the whole time with six students and talked to them one or two at a time. He had a real conversation with them and did not flit from one table to another as I do when I am giving a talk with a similar number of people. In fact, I gave a talk on my research on introvert/ambivert/extrovert leaders to a sim-ilar number of people in Iceland, where I hardly know a soul. I worked the room and connected with every table. But having watched Mr. Buffett the week before, I decided I needed to be a better leader and act like him and have some real in-depth conversation rather than just briefly connect with people. Yet another lesson learned from this great man. (Moore, 2017)

As someone who has grown to become an extrovert, I do find myself sometimes unnecessarily preoccupied with wanting to speak to everyone present to network and make contacts and privilege fleeting conversations over the deeper, more thoughtful ones, particularly at large-scale events. There is no 'right' way to interact with people when you are a leader, but it is important that allow students to see how introverts can make exceptionally strong leaders. Quiet and reflective leaders make a very worthy contribution to the world. Here is a summary of the reasons why:

- They are likely to be a fantastic listener and allow others to share their thoughts and plans

- They tend to analyse in amazing depth and detail by reading between and be-yond the lines

- Their preference for quiet solitude means that they might come up with some of the best ideas there are; creating, innovating, and planning come naturally to them

- They are self-reliant and well organised as they have learnt to trust their instincts and intuition

- They have deep, meaningful, and powerful relationships – these can serve them exceedingly well

- They can be excellent at coping with pressure and 'getting on with it'

There are no doubt more myths worthy of busting but for now all of the above suggest that there is no one-size-fits-all approach when it comes to leadership, at any stage in our lives. It is important to clarify, especially to young people embarking on their leadership journeys, that they rightfully belong in the realm of leadership. Dismantling the myths just discussed, and no doubt you have a list of your own, should be done early on and regularly reiterated if we wish our students to feel that sense of belonging and genuine confidence in their abilities.

Tool kit

- Find opportunities to talk about the nuances of leadership

- Look out for introverts and reluctant leaders and allow them to see beyond the leadership prototype

- Model listening to the ideas of others as good leadership practice

- Make students familiar with the idea of self-leadership

- Reassure students about any fears regarding public speaking

- Expose students to a range of role models with different leadership styles

- Create leadership roles that suit a range of personalities

- Keep conversations around leadership alive: don't just 'do' leadership

2 Values-based leadership

Read on to: explore the inextricable link between school values and conscious leadership while discovering powerful and enjoyable ways to convey this link to young people. Enjoy strategies for making values more visible and meaningful in the school day and for nurturing character building – minus the didacticism.

In Chapter 1, I dismantled some of the more popular and pervasive myths around leadership. Here, I focus much more on what leadership *is, should be, and could be*. Values are a good place to start in most aspects of life and make up the foundations that underpin our student leadership provision. No matter what the question, returning to values will give you some clue to the answer. I remind my students about the comforting power of strong values all the time. In a world that has begun to privilege 'wokeness' to such a degree [as it should!], values as a concept can sometimes appear old fashioned and traditionalist. I like to remind my students that mercifully, values will always be relevant and never go out of fashion. Our values are our guiding principles. They are what we keep coming back to when faced with inner conflict. They allow us to lead ourselves before we lead others.

'Values' as a term and concept can seem confusing and tenuous to young people; I assure you that observation is not meant condescendingly, as I would go so far as to suggest it is grey area for many adults too! It is a very worthwhile investment for schools to communicate the concept of values-based leadership to students, which will not only enhance their potential as leaders but also enable them to gain real clarity about the set of values they wish to privilege in their lives. Let me begin by delineating what values-based leadership looks like at schools.

What is values-based leadership?

Values-based leadership is the idea of drawing on your own core values and principles, alongside those of your team, and to consciously lead in accordance with them. Richard Barrett, author of *Building a Values-Driven Organisation*, describes it as "a way of making authentic decisions that builds trust and commitment" (Barrett, 2013). Doing this ensures that at every step of the way, you are leading with self-awareness and integrity to your fundamental values and beliefs. This is particularly valuable when it comes to difficult decision making, which may result in your decisions sometimes being unpopular, but nonetheless, always fair. We know that this is crucial when it comes to effective leadership – doing what is right, especially when it is not easy. It is my strong belief that young people are never too young to develop such a moral compass. Values-based leaders are open and transparent about communicating their values with clarity and purpose, in turn enabling others to develop and refine their own set of values. As this system expands, entire communities begin to grow and thrive, within schools and beyond. It is a system where leaders lead by example, living and breathing the values they promote in their biggest decisions to their smallest actions, and inspiring everyone to strive for self-growth. When our young leaders lead from a values-based approach, we can expect their choices to be grounded, well-considered, and fair. Their actions will benefit those they are responsible for leading, allow relationships of trust to be built, as well as set them off on a journey of self-discovery and growth. Values-based leadership allows young people to start asking questions such as "Who am I?", "What is important to me?", "How will my actions affect others?", and "What do I stand for?" – enabling them early on in life to think and act with resilience and purpose.

Once the concept of values-based leadership is understood by our students, along with the benefits it brings, we need to determine the values we wish to privilege. There is a catalogue worth of values if we seek to include them all and we stand to lose focus and purpose by casting our nets too widely. My recommendation is to carefully consider the context of our own institutions and communities to determine a set of values that become our framework. In my experience with young people, privileging the following values has been rewarding, and later on, I go into details about how to go about cultivating these in a school setting:

Compassion

Compassion lies at the very heart of good leadership, no matter who, where, and how many people one is leading. Unfortunately, the media – films and television in particular – have been guilty of portraying top-level leadership as ruthless and stony. Far too many CEOs are depicted as intimidating and fierce – and most definitely not approachable by a 'mere employee' (think of Bill Lumbergh from *Office Space* and Mr Burns from *The Simpsons*). It is important that we steer our young people away from viewing leadership as cold and harsh and nurture an understanding of the gains to be made from leading with kindness, empathy, and compassion. Behind compassionate leadership is an awareness of the lives and contexts of other people when leading them or working alongside them. Etymologically speaking, compassion is "Suffering together with another, participation in suffering; fellow-feeling, sympathy", suggesting that we need to learn quite early in life to relate with other individuals and take their circumstances into serious consideration when leading them (Sydney et al., 2015).

Creativity

The world is changing at an unprecedented rate, and it is increasingly challenging to predict what the future of information, connectivity, communication, and employment will look like over the next decade or so. Digitalisation will be at the heart of this future. The one certainty we do have is that leaders of the future will be traversing an exciting world, but a complex and unpredictable one, nonetheless. Perhaps one of the biggest changes we will see is the hyper-connectivity of a new world order, where keeping grounded and establishing perspective may feel challenging. In such times, leaders need to respond creatively; in the absence of templates, our young people will start from scratch and create templates of their own. They will try and test, create, and recreate. They will envision, imagine, innovate, invent – often in response to an unprecedent situation. Experiencing a global pandemic (COVID-19) has provided even further evidence that creative problem solving needs to front and centre in nurturing young leaders.

Courage

Courage has been hailed as the defining feature of great leaders, often distinguishing management from leadership. However, the concept of 'great leaders' can feel daunting, and to many, irrelevant and elusive. Even if the only person we ever end up leading is ourselves, courage is invaluable. The ability to take difficult decisions, to act on a life-long dream, to take a risk, to question, to call out injustices, to change a habit that no longer serves us: as schools we are in a powerful position to invite young people to show courage in a safe and supportive setting. We provide the safety net in which risk-taking can be encouraged in the knowledge that we can 'catch them if they fall'. Once established, the ability to feel and act with courage becomes contagious and inspires other individuals and whole teams to do the same.

Communication

My experience of working with hundreds of young people suggests to me that while they often have remarkable, valuable, and fascinating things to say, they don't always have the right tools to do this. By tools, I mean words, body language, sustained speech, eye contact, confidence, and clarity. Indeed, digital communication, social media, and texting have an important role to play here. The best leaders communicate with clarity, purpose, and passion, all of which we need to nurture in our young people. Whether it is a case of leading a small team, running an entire organisation, or maintaining successful relationships (both professional and personal), good communication is non-negotiable. When on the subject of communication, let's not forget the value of nurturing emotional literacy in our students. It took me three decades to develop the vocabulary to express my emotions effectively and I am still learning. What would I not have given to have exposure to this earlier in life, especially as a teenager? Emotional communication is not straight forward to teach and there is certainly no syllabus available for it, but there are methods that I have tried and tested which I say more about in Chapter 10.

Care

The value of care is incredibly ubiquitous in its application. Mr Manning, Head Teacher at St. Birinus, talks about care, one of the three core values of the school, with great passion and conviction. He draws examples from the care we take in our appearance, the presentation of our work, the words we use, and our demeanour around the school site. The best leaders will care about the well-being of others; about helping their team grow; about ethical working conditions; the environment and the impact of their words and actions on others. It is difficult to bring this list to a hasty conclusion. Where young people are concerned, however, I cannot stress enough the importance of nurturing habits of self-care and positivity. Self-care has been misconstrued as a selfish undertaking for far too long, not to mention the irony of caring for others while feeling depleted yourself. The more we talk about self-care, the better we role model it, the greater our chance of nurturing a wholesome and mentally well generation ahead of us, and there is much more on this in Chapter 9.

Commitment

I talk to my students about commitment a great deal: from starting out with the first sentence in an essay with a view to committing to the rest, applying for a student leadership position and committing to the responsibilities it entails, or committing to something more abstract, like self-growth or risk-taking. As Neil Strauss says, "Without commitment, you cannot have depth in anything, whether it's a relationship, a business or a hobby" (Strauss, 2007). And it is this depth that we need now, more than ever before, to cultivate in our young people. With technology in their pockets at most times and information available at their fingertips, the urge to explore anything in depth has been drastically reduced. The price to pay for the immediate gratification and speedy technology is the reassuring steadiness of long-term commitment. Technology is not going away anywhere and along with the immense positives it brings, it also brings distractions of vibrations, notifications, beeps, and flashes. We have a responsibility to teach our students about staying committed in a heady and distracted world.

Consider these a starting point if you like. Be flexible in your approach to values, as different situations will call forth different values-based leader responses. It is tempting to latch on to one value and stay stubbornly tethered to it. I have taught in schools and colleges in three different continents and have seen this too often: school leaders clinging to one or two values to a point where they begin to lose traction with young people. I have seen an over-emphasis on the value of resilience, for instance, which has meant that staff and students become weary and uninterested by the concept. Resilience is important but certainly not the answer in all situations. They don't want to hear about it any further and can anticipate with dread it being brought yet again in assembly. Keeping our values dynamic and eclectic means that our young people will feel motivated to live and act by them. It will allow them to think responsively and creatively and to develop empathy for the values privileged by those around them. As future leaders, they are likely to make choices that they are comfortable with, have more trusting relationships and by leading from a place of authenticity, be more cognisant of their inner selves.

In addition to the above, the attributes of self-reflection, introspection, grace, humility, open-mindedness, generosity, flexibility all count tremendously. I never shy away from using the language of values and character with my students, despite the suggestion that they have an old-fashioned ring to them. Leading with a strong set of values in place is our best chance at growing ourselves, while enabling and encouraging the growth of others. There is much we can do to instil in our young people the courage to be authentic.

The leadership ladder

How can we find ways to convey these values to our young people without it becoming either didactic or too simplistic? Assemblies, while powerful, have their limits, and with the best will in the world, we cannot have 'corridor conversations' with every pupil in our schools. At the Trust, we offer a system called *The Leadership Ladder* as an entitlement for all students as soon as they join us in Year 7, and it takes them through to Year 11. It is our top way of ensuring that all students in our care engage with leadership in a formal and strategic way and are recognised and rewarded for it. I want to share the planning behind this system with you, as well as demonstrate its practical application at school. On the front page of The Leadership Ladder booklet, we say the following:

Values-based leadership is a core aspect of our ethos at Didcot Girls' School. The Leadership Ladder has become a cherished tradition that enables us to fulfil our mission statement: We are a vibrant school community which empowers girls to become resilient and to fulfil their potential as future leaders. Young leadership is at the heart of our wider school provision, and we are committed to offering our students with every opportunity to grow, thrive and flourish into the change makers of the future. The Leadership Ladder is an entitlement for our Year 7 to Year 10 students and will prepare them for the many leadership roles we offer to our Year 11 students and Didcot Sixth Form. The provision is based on the values we cherish and uphold at DGS and offers a full range of eclectic opportunities for young people to embrace leadership in a way that they enjoy. There are different criteria for each year group, which will result in the following awards: Bronze, Silver, Gold and Platinum.

At its most basic level, The Leadership Ladder is based on the following three-pronged approach:

Values and Ethos of our school
Practical opportunities explicitly linked to our values
Celebration of involvement and achievement

How it works

Figure 2.1 Leadership ladder.

The DGS Leadership Ladder

Valued-based leadership is a core aspect of our ethos at Didcot Girls' School. The Leadership Ladder is a cherished tradition that enables us to fulfil our mission statement*: We are a vibrant school community which empowers girls to become resilient and to fulfil their potential as future leaders.* The Leadership Ladder is an entitlement for our **Year 7 to Year 10** students and will prepare them for the many leadership roles we offer to our Year 11 students and Didcot Sixth Form. There are different criteria for each year group, which will result in the following awards: Bronze, Silver, Gold and Platinum.

Values and Ethos of our school

Practical opportunities explicitly linked to our values

Celebration of involvement and achievement

How it works

The leadership ladder is based on the values we privilege and cherish at DGS – from resilience and courage to creativity, compassion and teamwork. If you are in Year 7 and 8 you will work towards Lower Bronze, Silver and Gold. At each level, you must complete 6 leadership activities to receive your award, which will be presented in the form of a badge in an assembly at the end of term. Your form tutor or the member of staff running the activity can sign the leadership ladder for you. The Platinum is a community-based award, where you contribute to your community; this award can be earned at any stage of your school life and is an excellent way for you to embrace the spirit of 'giving back'.

Notes

- Tutors will visit the Leadership Ladder booklet regularly with students
- Students to inform tutors when they have completed 6 activities
- An entitlement for Bronze and Silver; Gold encouraged but optional
- The Reading Bingo Cards are available in the student planner

Our Values

Resilience: The ability to adapt and grow following adversity/set backs

Respectful Relationships: the ability and intention to form wholesome relationships based on respect for others and ourselves

Communication/oracy: The ability to articulate our thoughts, needs and views in a clear, effective way

Compassion: the ability to relate with other individuals and treat them with kindness and consideration

Courage: the ability to work outside your comfort zone; to take difficult decisions, try new things and call out injustices

Creativity: the willingness to try things differently; to imagine, envision, innovate, and recreate

Integrity: the quality of being honest and having strong moral principles

Inclusivity: to recognise the worth and dignity of all people, irrespective of their colour, race, religion, gender or sexual orientation. To embrace and celebrate diversity in all its forms.

Growth Mindset: the belief that abilities and skills can be improved through dedication, determination and hard work

Commitment to excellence: the quality of being dedicated to a cause, activity or ambition with a view to completing it successfully

Teamwork: the ability to work well in teams, showing respect for the views and positions of others

Self-care & Wellbeing: the idea that we need invest time and effort in our emotional and mental well-being by being mindful of our nutrition, fitness and workload

Lower School Bronze Leadership Award

*Complete **6 actions** and get staff signatures to achieve your Bronze Leadership Award*

	Activity	Leadership Value	Date Completed	Staff Signature
1.	Lead a group/activity in a lesson	Confidence		
2.	Attend at least 10 sessions of a lunch/after school club	Courage/Commitment to Excellent		
3.	Be a Form Captain, School Council Rep or member of Year Group committee	Courage/Teamwork		
4.	Be recognised for showing acts of kindness to others	Compassion/Integrity		
5.	Participate in a House activity or competition	Teamwork		
6.	Participate in a school fixture/represent the school	Teamwork		
7.	Be recognised for excellent standards in uniform, punctuality and behaviour	Integrity/ Commitment to Excellent		
8.	Reading: I have completed the KS3 Reading Apprentice Bingo card	Reading for Pleasure		
9.	Expand your knowledge and understanding of other cultures by watching Ted Talks, reading articles, or listening to podcasts	Inclusivity (Specify what you have read, watched, heard – at least 3)		
10.	Worked exceptionally hard on…	Growth Mindset		
11.	Sought help when struggling with something	Resilience		
12.	Contribute to lessons	Oracy		
13.	Unplugged from devices for one hour each evening for at least 2 weeks	Wellbeing & Self Care		
14.	Complete Unifrog tasks	Employability Task		
15.	Participate in an out of school Takeover Challenge	Employability Task		

	Date	Signed
Bronze Badge Achieved		

Lower School Silver Leadership Award

*Complete **6 actions** and get staff signatures to achieve your Silver Leadership Award*

	Activity	Leadership Value	Date Completed	Staff Signature
1.	Made a presentation or speech in a lesson using high standards of oracy	Confidence		
2.	Worked towards raising awareness/funds for a school charity	Teamwork		
3.	Be a Form Captain, School Council Rep or member of Year Group committee	Courage/Integrity		
4.	Be a subject/reading ambassador	Commitment to Excellence		
5.	Give a talk to parents/primary school students at open event	Courage/Communication/Oracy		
6.	Recognised by a member of staff for being supportive to a peer	Compassion		
7.	Commit to a co-curricular activity or club	Commitment to Excellence		
8.	Reading: I have completed the KS3 Reading Journeyman Bingo card	Reading for Pleasure		
9.	Make a sustained effort to learn something new (cooking, gardening, sewing, language, sport)	Creativity/Wellbeing & Self Care		
10.	I am glad I made that mistake	Growth Mindset		
11.	Worked exceptionally hard on…	Growth Mindset		
12.	Participate in a wider school lunchtime/after school event	Commitment to Excellence/Teamwork		
13	Acted as a buddy to a Year 7 student	Compassion		
14	Recognised by a member of staff for significant improvement in digital literacy/online communication	Growth Mindset/Communication		
15.	Audition for a solo role in a school concert.	Courage		
16.	Complete Unifrog tasks	Employability Task		
17.	Participate in an in-school Takeover Day role	Employability Task		

	Date	Signed
Silver Badge Achieved		

Lower School Gold Leadership Award

*Complete **8 actions** and get staff signatures to achieve your Gold Leadership Award*

	Activity	Leadership Value	Date Completed	Staff Signature
1.	Help lead/play a part in a drama, dance or music show (in or outside school)	Confidence/ Teamwork		
2.	Present to governors/staff/parents	Communication/Courage		
3.	Be a Form Captain, Sports Captain School Council Rep or member of Year Group committee	Commitment to Excellence /Respectful Relationships		
4.	Plan and deliver part of a year group/House assembly	Communication/Courage		
5.	Be recognised by a member of staff for being an inspiration to others	Commitment to Excellence		
6.	Be recognised by a member of staff for using revision skills effectively over a sustained period of time	Commitment to Excellence /Responsibility		
7.	Invest time and effort in completing a display board/visual feature in school	Creativity		
8.	Reading: I have completed the KS3 Reading Champion Bingo card	Reading for Pleasure		
9.	Invested in my wellbeing by taking up a physical activity outside school for at least two weeks	Creativity/Wellbeing & Self-care		
10.	Learnt an important lesson from a set back and used it to grow and improve	Growth Mindset/Resilience		
11.	Recognised by a member of staff for being responsible, punctual, and polite	Commitment to Excellence		
12.	Recognised by your tutor for being an active and supportive member of the tutor group over at least 2 terms	Inclusivity/Respectful Relationships		
13	Worked alongside Climate Change and/or Diversity Leaders on a wider school project	Inclusivity/Teamwork		
14	Led a whole class/small group starter/section in PE	Courage/Growth Mindset		
15.	Be recognised by the Music Department for outstanding attendance and commitment to at least one ensemble across two terms.	Commitment to Excellence/Courage (Signed by member of Music Department)		
16.	On Unifrog: Record at least 6 competencies and at least 5 activities	Employability Task		

	Date	Signed
Gold Badge Achieved		

Upper School Bronze Leadership Award

*Complete **6 actions** and get staff signatures to achieve your Bronze Leadership Award*

	Activity	Leadership Value	Date Completed	Staff Signature
1.	Help to lead a lunchtime/after school club for one term	Teamwork/Courage		
2.	Helped to organise or performed in a Drama/Dance/Music concert or production	Teamwork/Courage		
3.	Work with students from lower years for at least one term	Inclusivity/Respectful Relationships		
4.	Be recognised by a member of staff for being consistently responsible, punctual and polite	Integrity/ Commitment to Excellence		
5.	Reading: complete the KS4 Reading Apprentice Bingo Card	Reading for Pleasure		
6.	Serve the role of a community prefect	Courage		
7.	Invest in your wellbeing by taking up an after-school activity for at least 4 weeks	Wellbeing & Self care		
8.	Plan and speak in at least 2 assemblies over the year	Confidence		
9.	Be recognised for participating in class discussions regularly and respectfully	Commitment to Excellence /Growth Mindset		
10.	Using revisions tools and skills to consolidate learning consistently	Commitment to Excellence		
11.	Be recognised by your tutor for having a positive attitude and showing resilience over a term	Resilience		
12.	Invest in digital well-being by going device free for one hour each day for a month	Wellbeing & Selfcare		
13	Be involved in planning or participating in a House event	Teamwork		
14	Be recognised for an achievement outside school (music, sport, publishing, competition etc)	Commitment to Excellence/Creativity		
15	On Unifrog: Record Competencies, at least 10 Record Activities, at least 8	Employability Task		
16	Participate in an out of school Takeover Challenge	Employability Task		

	Date	Signed
Bronze Badge Achieved		

Upper School Silver Leadership Award

*Complete **6 actions** and get staff signatures to achieve your Silver Leadership Award*

	Activity	Leadership Value	Date Completed	Staff Signature
1.	Represent the school in a competition or event	Confidence/Teamwork		
2.	Work closely with the House Captain Team to organise an event	Commitment/Teamwork		
3.	Be a Form Captain, School Council Rep or member of Year Group committee	Courage/Commitment to Excellence		
4.	Plan and deliver at least 3 house/year group assemblies over a year	Confidence/Creativity		
5.	Present at least twice to governors/staff/parents over the year	Courage/Communication/Oracy		
6.	Raise awareness over a significant issue, working alongside Climate Change, Charity, Diversity Leaders	Creativity/Inclusivity/Courage		
7.	Commit to a co-curricular activity for at least two terms (choose from our wide list of clubs)	Commitment to Excellence		
8.	Reading: I have completed the KS4 Reading Journeyman Bingo card	Reading for Pleasure		
9.	Take sustained action to be environmentally friendly at school and home	Integrity/Wellbeing & Selfcare		
10.	I have taken steps outside my comfort zone and embraced challenges	Growth Mindset		
11.	Worked exceptionally hard on...	Growth Mindset		
12.	Become an Ethos Leader or be part of the Year 10 House Captain Team	Courage/Teamwork		
13.	Be recognised by staff for sustained commitment to co-curricular groups by participating in at least two Dance/Drama/Music productions or concerts.	Commitment to Excellence /Courage		
14.	Taken part in a mock interview	Employability Task		
15.	On Unifrog: I have completed a CV	Employability Task		

	Date	Signed
Silver Badge Achieved		

*Complete **8 actions** and get staff signatures to achieve your Gold Leadership Award*

	Activity	Leadership Value	Date Completed	Staff Signature
1.	Regularly plan and deliver assemblies	Confidence to Excellence		
2.	Lead a club for younger students	Teamwork/Inclusivity		
3.	Help organise a whole school event, campaign, or competition	Commitment to Excellence/Teamwork		
4.	Be appointed on the Year 11 Leadership Team	Courage/commitment		
5.	Represent the school at an event, fixture, or competition	Courage/Resilience		
6.	Recognised by a member of staff for representing school values consistently	Integrity/Respectful Relationships/Resilience		
7.	Reading: I have completed the KS4 Reading Champion Bingo card	Reading for Pleasure		
8.	Played a part in organizing IWD Student Leadership Conference	Teamwork		
9.	Worked closely to help a younger student over a number of weeks (academically or pastorally)	Compassion/Respectful Relationships		
10.	I am gone above and beyond in a subject...	Growth Mindset		
11.	I have used my resilience to invest time and effort in a subject I struggle with	Resilience		
12.	I have achieved something significant outside school...	Creativity/Growth Mindset		
13.	Recognised by a member of staff for outstanding digital skills	Communication		
14.	Be recognised by staff for a sustained commitment to co-curricular by performing in at least four Dance/Drama/Music productions or concerts.	Commitment to Excellence/Courage		
15.	Participated in Work Experience	Employability Task		
16.	Participate in an in school Takeover Day role	Employability Task		

	Date	Signed
Gold Badge Achieved		

Platinum Community Leadership Award

Aim: This is a chance for students to use their Leadership skills to volunteer in the community. Students can choose how they want to contribute – helping at a care home or charity, organised litter picking, raising funds for a charity or helping at previous primary schools are all great options.

How: Record your hours each week and ensure your community link signs them off. Take notes about your experience as your House Captains will ask you to reflect on this before you are awarded the badge.

Levels: 1=10 hours, 2=20 hours, 3=50 hours 4=100 hours

Examples:

- Helping a charity – run a fundraising event in your community for a local charity
- Community action – running a campaign to promote environmental/social issues
- Coaching – at your local sports/athletic clubs
- Helping people – at your local scout group/youth group
- Mentoring – regularly helping younger students at school

Timescale: You can complete any level over the course of the school year.

Platinum Community Leadership Award

Date and Hours Completed	Leadership Activity	Community Link Signature

Leadership Tracking Record

Once you have completed a stage make sure that you tell your tutor/relevant staff member who can then sign off the step.

Stage Completed	Date	Badge Received (Tick)
Lower Bronze		
Lower Silver		
Lower Gold		
Upper Bronze		
Upper Silver		
Upper Gold		
Platinum		

Our Mission Statement:

"We are a vibrant school community which empowers girls to become resilient and to fulfil their potential as future leaders."

The Leadership Ladder is an entitlement for Year 7 to Year 10 students, and we expect every student to undertake this exciting leadership journey with us. The ladder itself is based on the values we privilege and cherish at DGS – from resilience and courage to creativity, kindness and teamwork. From these values we create a full range of eclectic opportunities for young people to embrace and enjoy. If you are in Year 7 and 8 you will work towards Lower Bronze, Silver and Gold. At each level, you must complete 6 leadership activities to receive your award, which will be presented in the form of a badge in an assembly at the end of term. Over the years, our students have worn these badges with great pride on their blazers. Your form tutor or the member of staff running the activity can sign the leadership ladder for you. The Platinum is a community-based award, where you contribute to your community for a number of hours; this award can be earned at any stage of your school life and is an excellent way for you to embrace the spirit of 'giving back'. The Platinum award is very prestigious and students have always enjoyed getting involved in it. We hope that students will enjoy growing their leadership skills with our exciting provision (Figure 2.1).

Notes

- *Tutors will visit the Leadership Ladder booklet regularly with students*

- *Students to inform tutors when they have completed 6 activities*

- *The leadership ladder will prepare students for the leadership roles in Year 11*

- *An entitlement for Bronze and Silver; Gold encouraged but optional*

The booklet goes on to capture a sample of some of the values we espouse (wording taken from booklet):

Resilience: *the ability to adapt and grow following adversity/setbacks*

Respectful Relationships*: the ability and intention to form wholesome relationships based on respect for others and ourselves*

Communication/oracy: *the ability to articulate our thoughts, needs and views in a clear, effective way*

Compassion: *the ability to relate with other individuals and treat them with kindness and consideration*

Courage: *the ability to work outside your comfort zone; to take difficult decisions, try new things and call out injustices*

Creativity: *the willingness to try things differently; to imagine, envision, innovate, and recreate*

Integrity: *the quality of being honest and having strong moral principles*

Inclusivity: *to recognise the worth and dignity of all people, irrespective of their colour, race, religion, gender or sexual orientation. To embrace and celebrate diversity in all its forms.*

Growth Mindset: the belief that abilities and skills can be improved through dedication, determination and hard work

Commitment to excellence: the quality of being dedicated to a cause, activity or ambition with a view to completing it successfully

Teamwork: the ability to work well in teams, showing respect for the views and positions of others

Self-care & Wellbeing: the idea that we need invest time and effort in our emotional and mental well-being by being mindful of our nutrition, fitness and workload

It's about the launch, the communication, the WHY. It's also about making it eclectic, varied, and differentiated enough for everyone to partake and enjoy. A natural way to allow everyone to be part of the leadership journey in their own ways. And a wonderful way to capture our values without being too prescriptive. It works online and needs some admin and tutor support. Tracking allows us to know where the gaps are with our spotlight students too.

The Platinum Award: This is a chance for students to take their leadership outside the school community into the wider community. Students can choose how they want to contribute – helping at a care home or charity, organised litter picking, raising funds for a charity, or helping at previous primary schools. Hours are recorded and awards given after a presentation. This allows that leadership journey to keep moving forward. I recently asked Chloe Cormack, currently Head Girl at Sixth Form and our Associate Head Girl last year, to talk to me about her experiences with the Platinum Award. Here is how the conversation went:

Chloe, could you start by telling me what appealed to you about the Platinum Award?

The Platinum Award felt to me like the obvious next challenge. I have always loved volunteering within the community, so I wanted to get involved straight away. I feel that in Years 7 and 8, there is enthusiasm to volunteer, but this often fades away as we move up the year groups. The Platinum Award provides a platform to keep going; it provides that 'nudge'.

What steps did you take to start working towards the Platinum Award?

I scoped out places that are most likely to need volunteers and made enquiries about the kind of work they might need. Speaking to older students and family members helped me to narrow down this list to places that appealed to me most. Volunteering at your local primary school is always a good place to start, particularly on INSET (In-Service Education and Training) days, when my own school is closed for students.

Which aspects of this work were most enjoyable and what did you learn along the way?

The most enjoyable aspect of the Platinum Leadership Award has been to volunteer at my primary schools and 'give back' to teachers who did such an incredible amount for me. That has been truly gratifying. This work has taught me about compassion, communication, and empathy. Working alongside a boy with special educational needs was especially valuable as I learnt about pace and tone when communicating. The rewards for 'doing something for nothing' are immense and the Platinum Award allows us to experience this over a full five years.

You have a minute to convince younger students to strive for Platinum. What would you say?

Science proves that volunteering in the local community benefits not just others but is brilliant for boosting our own well-being and self-esteem. If we ever needed another reason to contribute time and effort to a good cause, surely this is it! The world needs positive actions now more than ever before so get involved and you will love it!

Armed with an authentic understanding of the link between values and leadership, we are on our way towards nurturing conscious and compassionate leaders who will develop their own set of values and learn to stay aligned with them. Individual strong values eventually come together to create a culture of inclusion and positivity, where people feel appreciated and motivated. Ultimately, we can tether just about everything we do in schools to our consciously lived values.

Tool Kit:

● Ensure staff and students understand what values-based leadership is, and why it is so important

● Delineate your top values, and share them with the school community regularly

● Find creative school-wide ways to expose students to these values regularly

● Provide tangible ways for students to live by these values

● Allow students time and space to develop their own values

● Encourage students to take their leadership skills into the wider community

3 Equality, diversity, and inclusion

Read on to: find out about powerful, meaningful, and sustainable ways to create and nurture equality, diversity, and inclusion in our schools. Discover how Equality, Diversity and Inclusion (EDI) can look on a day-to-day basis and enable our entire school community to thrive. Balancing the 'why' with the 'how', this chapter offers plenty of exciting suggestions for a diverse and inclusive school culture.

Let me begin with a reminder: a culture of diversity and inclusion within our schools is focusing our energies on equality, diversity, and inclusion in schools is not just *the right thing to do*; sometimes, when we approach things with the attitude of, 'we must do this or we might be in trouble', the results are a little bit dry and uninspiring. Of course, prioritising diversity and inclusion in schools is the right thing to so, but it is also *the most moral, exciting, energising, and empowering thing to do*. In an ideal world, these are the reasons we should spend time talking about inclusion. In this chapter, I delineate the sorts of diversities schools should have on their minds when appointing student leadership teams as well organising their ethos calendars; I will also look in depth at what is involved in building our systems to mark socio-economic, ethnic, racial, and cognitive diversities in our schools. The notion of cognitive diversity and its emphasis on having an eclectic range of 'minds' on any leadership team is a relatively new one in schools, and I will be using some of Mathew Syed's research to present its significance in the school body. You can expect concrete advice on how to develop student leadership teams that are truly diverse and representative, as well as suggestions for how to meaningfully track student participation using pre-existing data with regard to Pupil Premium, Special Educational Needs & Disability (SEND), ethnic minorities, and religious minorities. The chapter will go into detail about how to engage these different groups, including advice on how to recruit a diverse range of guest

 DOI: 10.4324/9781003275985-3

speakers and role models; how to prepare a data tracking system; how to advertise leadership roles in order to generate interest across the student body. An important aspect of this chapter will be about making leadership accessible to a range of student personalities: your assertive, confident, and 'noisy' students as well as quiet, reflective, and sensitive learners. At the Ridgeway Education Trust, student leadership roles have been created over the years with immense thought and care – this has ensured that our student leadership teams are truly diverse and as a result have great impact in the school and the community.

The context/the 'why'

The AQA (Assessment and Qualifications Alliance) English Language paper provides students with a stimulus photograph each year, based on which students must write a descriptive piece. In past years, we have had images of busy sea sides, crowded fun fairs, tranquil beaches, and deserted streets at midnight, studded with bright streetlamps. It is a lovely opportunity for students to feel inspired, use their imaginations, and get happily carried away. As the final question on the exam paper, it can feel like freedom, after answering highly structured questions requiring close analysis of challenging extracts.

In the summer of 2022, as I write this, the image provided is that of a small Mexican kitchen, bright and colourful, walls studded with handicrafts, heavily patterned tablecloths, and intricately designed crockery. The image is traced back to an Airbnb property - no doubt one that proves immensely popular. To my mind, there is more to discover in this one photograph of a small Mexican kitchen than there is in several photographs combined. When I looked at it, I smiled with intrigue, curiosity, and relief that exam boards were finally looking beyond the reaches of the familiar. You would be right to begin questioning at this point the relevance of all this to a chapter on Equality, Diversity, and Inclusion.

The connection lies in the response this image elicited immediately after the exam. The image was met, largely speaking, with either annoyance or ridicule, both of which are highly telling. It did not make sense to people to be confronted with an image so unfamiliar and removed from their daily lives. What could they possibly say about it? Was it a hobbit home? How could the exam board do this? I came across hundreds of such responses, both in person and on social media platforms. Staff were cross too; they had not prepared their students for such an unexpected image.

Initially, these reactions frustrated me and left me feeling disillusioned. Eventually, however, I began to ask if we could really blame so many young people for reacting this way. Given diversity still feels so tokenistic in everyday life at so many schools and in so many homes, it is no surprise young people are stumped by an image like this. We need our young people to not just gain more exposure to different cultures and lives but to be more accommodating towards difference.

The reactions of our students don't come from a place of malice; they come from a place of ignorance. Ignorance is (mercifully) easier to right than malice: we need to place EDI at our schools front and centre. A few posters here and there, alongside a small box worth of content will not be enough; nor will ensuring the presence of the odd ethnic minority student on our brochures and other promotional material. We need to dig a lot deeper and there is no time to waste.

There has never been a greater need for schools to look inwards and examine closely how equal, diverse, and inclusive their provision really is. EDI is vital at all levels: Leadership and Management, Behaviour & Welfare, Teaching & Learning, and Personal Development. In this chapter, my focus is how to allow EDI to grow and thrive in the context of Personal Development, though I suggest strong links between this and Teaching & Learning.

Return to your mission statement

Through this book, I consciously repeat the idea of returning to our values and our mission statement. Not a day in my working week passes without me revisiting values with a student, colleague or indeed in my own thinking as I plan and reflect. It keeps me grounded to know that I am 'contained' (in the most positive and liberating sense of that word!) within parameters of what really matters – the beating hearts of our schools – our values. These parameters, paradoxically perhaps, allow me the freedom to keep improving and developing the ethos of our school. Within them, I can plan creatively and take risks without worrying, confident in the knowledge that I remain aligned with the core ethics and values of my school. To encapsulate all that is important to us in a mission statement, which by their very nature concise, is challenging but worthwhile. I believe EDI must be an authentic, core, and non-negotiable part of our mission statements – here is an example of what this looks like at our Trust:

We are committed to ensuring that equality diversity and inclusion are at the heart of the shared values at our school. There is a real passion from staff and students to develop our understanding of EDI and take our work in this area forward in a very visible and strategic way. (www.ridgewayeducationtrust. co.uk, n.d.)

Once our mission statement is in place and we believe in it wholeheartedly, we are ready to take this good work further, confident and reassured of our vision and purpose. I have not always thought about diversity within the school community as much as I have done in the past five years or so. Interestingly, this shift in focus was not the result of a game-changing epiphany but rather from a growing sense of frustration within our student body. It became palpable to us that something about the way we did things was not sitting comfortably with them. The unease manifested itself in various ways: students approaching me to ask what our plans for Eid or Diwali celebrations were members of the LGBTQIA+ (Abbreviation for Lesbian, Gay, Bisexual, Transgender, Queer, Intersex, and Asexual) plus community and allies questioning why homophobia was not regularly addressed within a narrative about anti-bullying approaches at school and members of our BAME (Black, Asian and Minority Ethnic) community pushing that we do more and say more - that we go beyond ticking boxes and doing what is required but no more. These suggestions began piling up and my response to them was at once defensive and apologetic. After each conversation, I was determined to put something in place, something concrete and tangible, that would satiate the sense of frustration that was being conveyed to me. I was approachable and responsive, but I didn't have a strategy. I needed to start thinking about how equality and diversity could become an integral and an extricable part of our ethos in a way that meant that we were always thinking about it and not reducing it to an agenda item add meetings and briefings. What follow are some examples of strategies I put in place that have become systemic over time.

Appointing a diverse student leadership team

I will begin by talking about diversity within our student leadership teams. I want to share here strategies for planning, appointing, training, and managing diverse and exciting student leadership team at schools. I will explore what a successful and thriving student leadership program can look and feel like, based on my eight years of experience in developing and improving student leadership provisions at secondary school level. You will find step-by-step approaches will be offered how to design leadership roles for young people bearing in mind different personalities, interests, and strength. Interview formats, including a range of potential questions that bring out the best in young people, will be provided; in-house training ideas for young leaders will be shared; and, perhaps more importantly, there will be concrete advice for how to get young people to achieve the most out of these roles. I will explain how a robust and thriving team of student leaders can serve as aspirational role models for the rest of the school and every level. I will suggest a range of activities, events, and initiatives, including our very popular Student Leadership Conference and House Opening Ceremony, that leadership teams can run throughout the year. The chapter will conclude with compelling evidence that the skills and knowledge that schools can disseminate to young leaders has a direct and powerful link to their futures.

The process

Unless we are careful at the very early stages of recruiting student leadership teams, it should not surprise us that our teams comprise a thoroughly predictable bunch. While there is nothing wrong with having a predictable bunch – we know they are keen and will deliver – can you imagine the number of young people we stand to exclude? This may be out of a fear of applying, an avoidance of exposure and failure, imposter syndrome, or the refusal to see themselves as future leaders. Whatever the reasons, we need to think cleverly about ways to pre-empt the reluctance at an early stage.

It is certainly worth thinking about timeframes when it comes to appointing your student leadership team. If you need your leaders in position for September, my advice is to begin the process in March. The first step will be advertising the roles and this process is best framed within regular, open, and inspiring discussions about young leadership. At the Trust, we arrange a morning for our outgoing Year 11 student leadership team to deliver an interactive workshop to our Year 10 students. The workshop serves as a powerful platform to answer questions about the roles, showcase the benefits of student leadership, and enable younger students to see themselves in leadership positions. In my experience, when these messages come from students instead of staff, their impact is multiplied manifold. Children's rights activist Marian Wright Edleman said: "you can't be what you can't see" and a face-to-face discussion with students only a year older, holding aspirational leadership roles will enable students to realise that they too can take on these responsibilities: that they belong (Milbrey Wallin Mclaughlin, 2018). The workshops are scaled down and held a few times over the course of the week to allow them to feel non-intimidating and comfortable; they can include energisers, icebreakers, and physical movement to create a sense of enjoyment. Essentially, the workshops serve to whet the appetites of future young leaders.

When designing the roles we make available, it is important to begin by thinking of young people and the aspects of school life that matter most to them. We must also make student leadership opportunities eclectic and accessible to a range of student personalities: our more 'typical' assertive, naturally confident, and "noisy" students, as well as quiet, reflective, and sensitive learners. The reminder that leadership is about leading themselves first and then others is a powerful one at this stage too, because by this logic no student should keep away on the basis of feeling that they 'belong'. I find that the public speaking aspect of leadership is a big one – this is worth really clarifying to students as they should not hold back from applying just because they don't feel confident to speak in public – there are a lot of other roles and significant responsibilities they can have. I understand that anxiety and fear will stop a number of young people from sticking their necks out for these roles and this is genuinely a shame, because chances are there is a part of them that wants to experience it immensely. It's about drawing out these held-back individuals who are overthinking their ability to lead. Also, of course, there are no guarantees that all students are getting the encouragement and motivation at home so as a school we have an even greater responsibility to encourage and engage young people inclusively. Assemblies and visits to tutor time are effective ways of speaking openly to students about the barriers to leadership. We need to tell them explicitly:

- You have it within you to be a leader

- You can pick a role either big or small; there are many options

- This opportunity will help your confidence grow

- Working in a team is great for your well-being

- Be proactive: seek help if you are unsure about filling the application form

- Do you have a vision for your school community? This opportunity may help you take that vision forward

When it comes to ensuring your student leadership team is as diverse as possible, think carefully about the diversities you wish to have represented – race, ethnicity, sexual orientation, religion, disability, special needs, socio-economic status, and cognitive diversity all need to be considered. In the years to follow, this somewhat mechanical approach to leadership will, we hope, no longer be necessary. For now, however, the more carefully we approach diversity, the better our chances of being fully inclusive. I have found it particularly useful to liaise with the SEND department to ensure that we are working collaboratively to create a truly diverse student leadership team. Not only will these leaders represent SEND, but they also always make hugely important contributions, bringing in unique and valuable perspectives to a team, often perspectives that we may have overlooked. Once appointed, participation should be tracked to establish where and why there are gaps and identify the steps that need to be taken to fill them.

At the Trust, student leadership roles have been created over the years with immense thought and care. This has ensured that our student leadership teams are truly diverse and have great impact in the school and wider community. We make no apology about appointing a healthy number of young leaders. Some may see this as detracting from the exclusivity of leadership – well, that is the point!

Here are a few more points to bear in mind:

- Advertising and publicising through all means available to us is important: in assemblies, tutor time, letters home, social media platforms, etc.

- Encouragement, particularly of students who are in any way disadvantaged (race analogy) needs to be offered along the way.

- To make the process fair and equitable, we should be able to accept applications both electronically and as paper copies.

- It is always best to interview as many candidates as possible. This experience itself will be a powerful learning opportunity for our students.

- Liaising with your Careers Lead and having them support students with writing an excellent application is always beneficial. This could take the form of an assembly, a tutor session, or a drop-in workshop style session.

- Design your interview questions to bring out the best in pupils and not to 'catch them out'.

- Have a friendly, robust, and enabling interview panel: try to include pastoral, teaching, and non-teaching staff for the best coverage.

- Look for what is promising in each candidate and think carefully about which positions fit them best. Sometimes, we are in a better position to assess this than they are.

- It is best not to leave it too late to announce the results of the interview, and as with other jobs, it is important to offer feedback to those who didn't get appointed.

- To make the process as professional as possible, and give students a taste of success, I always send a congratulatory letter home to parents or carers.

- It is important to find a suitable time in assembly to announce the new team and give them a chance to introduce themselves. This is also a good time to hand out badges and ties, etc., depending on the system at your school.

- The newly appointed student leadership team should have a very clear sense of the roles and responsibilities they can expect to have.

- I like to organise a 'training morning', where we can offer icebreaking challenges, safeguarding training, planning time, and perhaps inspiration from a guest speaker.

Diversity and leadership

I want to say a little more about the process of sharing leadership roles with students as well as being clear about what these roles will entail through the course of the year. This provides students with the knowledge and confidence they need to take the first step and apply. When we leave them guessing or worried, the 'what if's' come in the way and we potentially miss out on receiving applications from some excellent candidates. From experience, the more clarity and reassurance we offer in the early stages, the more chances we have of students coming forward. Here are some examples of the leadership opportunities we offer at the Trust:

Sixth Form Executive (a group of student leaders who hold responsibilities for various areas of school life including well-being, sports, climate action, charity, social events, etc.) Much more on this in Chapter 11, which is dedicated exclusively to ethos in the Sixth Form.

Head Students

Charity Leaders

Diversity Leaders

Climate Action Leaders

Well-being Officers

Ethos Leaders

Community Prefects

I believe that expanding the number of leadership roles available to young people is an important first step: this will go a long way in eliciting a diverse range of individual strengths.

The process of application is best kept simple and straightforward, starting out with an application form that a student can fill entirely independently (see example below). The process of applications should be as transparent as possible too; get as many staff involved possible, both teaching and non-teaching. Get your input from the SEND teams too. Asking for staff endorsement has meant that not only are students showing initiative and willing in seeking these out, but staff also have a way to expressing their input. Additionally, provide plenty of assurance to students that training both in house and external will be provided – they certainly don't have to know everything and have all the skills in advance or be fully prepared.

Job description – House Captain

"Leadership is the capacity to translate vision into reality."

The roles of House and Deputy House Captain are ones of privilege, pride, and responsibility.

They are more than just a title and badge and require dedication and commitment for an entire year.

Characteristics of a House Captain

Someone with a vision and ambition

Someone who believes in and embodies the Growth Mindset

Polite and well-mannered

Organised and committed

Confident, articulate, and well spoken

Respectful and tolerant

Resilient

Well-presented in uniform and appearance

Able to liaise and converse with staff, students, and the wider community

Act responsibly and be a role model for other students

You can expect

Responsibilities appropriate to the position of House Captain or Deputy House Captain

Full support from staff to organise events and teams

Time to meet as a House Captain Team

Assembly time

Ownership of House notice board

Plan and lead the annual Year 9 Leadership Conference

To plan interesting and stimulating assemblies and deliver them confidently.

To host termly celebration breakfasts for students who have made an exceptional contribution to House activities.

To invite House namesakes to school for presentations and talks.

We expect you

To be a positive role model and ambassador for the school.

To be enthusiastic and committed to the House System at Didcot Girls' School.

To creatively develop and enhance the existing House System

To be friendly and positive with **all students**, particularly within your House.

To be part of the team of House Captains who work together to achieve success for all.

To work to deadlines.

Responsible to

List of staff members

Name of applicant: Tutor Group:

Please fill out this form (using blue or black pen) and return to your tutors no later than (Date and Time)

Briefly describe why you are suitable for this role:

Describe some of the leadership qualities you have demonstrated in your school life so far:

What do you hope to gain from this role?

Describe any two new House initiatives you would launch in this role:

Please name two members of staff (teaching or non-teaching) as your **Referees**. Please ensure that you speak to them before putting their names down. 1. 2.	I would like to be considered for the role of Prefect if I am not successful in my House Captain application: Yes _____ No _____ (Tick as appropriate)

Equality, diversity, and inclusion focus groups

In addition to making our student leadership teams as diverse and inclusive as we can, there is a lot else we can put into place as schools to promote equality and diversity in our institutions. One thing I successfully initiated a few years ago is a large focus group from across the Trust, which we call the EDI Steering Committee, established with the aim of promoting inclusivity and diversity in all aspects of our school community. It felt like a logical first step: a group of likeminded people, representing the staff and student body, determined to make the school more inclusive and equal with a view to leaving the institution better than they found it. At the Trust, this group meet termly with a predetermined agenda. These have included working towards improving our website to reflect the diversity of our school community, changing the house namesakes to become more inclusive (at the time of writing, we have six white women as our namesakes), creating a logo for EDI, diversifying the curriculum, planning multicultural days, and collating pupil voice. It's important to involve students and even invite them to lead these sessions and minute them, where possible. At the Trust, it has served as an excellent opportunity for staff and students to come together and air their views in a wholesome environment. I hold these EDI Steering Committee meetings in our very welcoming school library, which is reassuringly well stocked with thousands of books representing thousands of voices. It feels like the perfect setting to explore how we can widen the reaches of our minds and make time to listen to a range of voices.

As schools, we have a unique opportunity to prepare our young people for the diversity, which they will undoubtedly encounter in the world of work ahead, and in doing this, empower them to thrive in these diverse teams and environments. Organisations worldwide are expecting their employees to work cross collaboratively, often with an international dimension. Deborah D. Hazzard, clinical Associate Professor and Associate Dean of Diversity and Inclusion at the University of South Carolina's Darla Moore School of Business says, "If we want to prepare our students to engage successfully in the workplace, then they need to have team engagement experiences". She adds that

> Given demographic trends and the rise of global corporations, workplace teams will likely be increasingly diverse. As professors, we can prepare our students for this reality with team assignments that provide opportunities to learn how to engage effectively across differences.

Hazzard also makes the case that

> People who work in diverse teams tend to do a better job considering multiple stakeholder perspectives and using a broader lens when solving problems. They are more mindful of their own biases and willing to consider

other perspectives. As a result, they may be able to reach better outcomes by developing more informed, thoughtful, and innovative solutions.

Hazard posits a difference in the dimensions of diversity she considers when creating student leadership teams: "internal dimensions" of diversity which includes aspects such as race and gender as well as "external dimensions" of diversity which reflects socio-economic positions and cognitive differences (Deborah D. Hazzard and Catherine Peyrols Wu).

At the Trust, we spend a lot of time dismantling stereotypes, which young people (and indeed older ones!) pick up unwittingly and struggle to shrug off. I have already talked about how diverse student leadership teams go a long way in the dismantling process by focusing on individuals rather than groups or 'types'. We increasingly ensure that we have representation in terms of personalities, beliefs, experiences, strengths, and ideas, to get a truly diverse range of young people around the table. This diversity will reap tremendous rewards, but care must be taken to offer scaffolding and support in those early weeks and months where standards are being set and relationships are being built. We become so accustomed to spending time with and making decisions alongside likeminded individuals that the wonderful diversity of these teams might seem challenging and obstructive to begin with. It is worth investing time in talking explicitly about diversity and inclusion, as well as facilitating meetings and planning slots until an ease develops within the group and they begin to naturally gel. It's worth adding that for these teams to feel not just diverse but also inclusive, it's important to be open about respect, politeness, acceptance, and inclusion from the very start. Without this, we risk further marginalisation and 'othering', very much defeating the purpose of what we have set out to achieve. The idea is for all voices to be valued, heard, and respected even where opinions clash.

Capturing diversity in school life

Once the structures are in place for EDI to thrive, we can begin thinking about how this culture can be reflected in a visible and tangible way around school. This responsibility falls in the first instance with our EDI Steering Committee, who, even as I write this, are working hard to plan the annual programme for 'Culture Week'. Even at a young age, they are mindful that diversity is not built in a week, and they are very weary of anything that feels 'tickboxy' and contrived, but the energy, vitality, vibrance, joy, and appreciation of cultures this week brings about is invaluable in our school year. They are conscious of culture becoming reductive or too easy; they appreciate that some aspects of the week can become tolerant of cultural appropriation. This awareness in itself is powerful. It is not perfection we seek but awareness and the will to change the status quo; events such as Culture Week, year after year, can bring about awareness and curiosity amongst our young people in a most enjoyable way.

So how does Culture Week work? Planning and strategising well in advance are the keys to success here. Each year, we look carefully through our data and determine which cultures we will explore in the week. Ideally, we would celebrate all cultures, as they are all magnificently exciting, but alas this is a practical impossibility and so we are responsive and change our selection each year. Throughout the week, we see an eclectic range of activities unfold. Form time is used to offer an enjoyable and engaging introduction to the countries and cultures we celebrate, and our student leaders prepare resources that cover music, dance, languages, geography, history, religions, politics, and international relations.

Furthermore, each day of the week is dedicated to a school-wide event: examples include The Great School Recipe Swap – what better way, after all, to develop an understanding and appreciation of cultures than by food? The recipes are compiled into a book that is then shared with the school community – a reminder of just how wonderfully diverse we are. Another idea is to host a non-uniform day which is an invitation to wear something that captures the culture we are associated with most, and we encourage both historical and traditional as well as modern interpretations of this. It is an opportunity to appreciate, enjoy, and respect clothes and accessories from a range of cultures. There is a day for music and a day for dance, making the week one to look forward to with great anticipation. At the Trust, Culture Week culminates in a large-scale event called 'Culture Evening', where we have a host of mesmerising performances from exceptionally talented students followed by delicious foods to sample from around the globe. It is wholesome, fantastically entertaining, and goes a long way in enabling all our students to feel 'seen'.

Religious festivals also provide a wonderful opportunity to us to celebrate the diversity within our school communities and we should be making the most of these. To give an example, 11% of our student body comprises students from Muslim households; many of our students fast through the holy month of Ramadan. Just before the month of Ramadan begins, we send out a letter to all our families, not just the Muslim families. Here is a sample written by our Head Teacher, Georgina Littler:

Dear Parents and Carers

Re: Ramadan

We felt it would be useful to advise all parents of the arrangements and support the school offer in this season of Ramadan, as well as ask for your support in ensuring we are as well informed as possible in order to ensure the best possible provision for all students.

We are committed to the welfare of all of our students and able to offer several important adjustments to the school day and lessons for any students observing the fast. Equally, we are aware that some school functions and commitments can be inconvenient for families during Ramadan and alternative arrangement may be possible. We are aware that parents may have concerns regarding Year 11 assessments about to take place. Please do let us know if you have any queries regarding these and students who may be fasting.

Firstly, we recognise that, as Ramadan falls in the warmer months, some students may need to be mindful of their involvement in physically-demanding tasks. The PE department are prepared and experienced in supporting fasting students and will monitor students carefully, allowing regular rest breaks and shelter from the sun if necessary. Similarly, other teachers whose lessons require physical exertion or exposure to the sun are prepared to make adjustments where necessary. In order to support us with this, you may wish to let your daughter's Head of Year know that your daughter is fasting and that they may need support and monitoring in PE or other activities.
If it becomes necessary to sit out of any activities, we will arrange proper supervision and, where possible, provide work to ensure the time is well-used.

We do, however, know that it is important to many Muslims that the fast does not impede their day-to-day activities and we are happy to support students who choose to continue to participate fully. Rest assured that we will not force students to reduce their involvement or not engage in activities unless there is a concern for their health and welfare.

Secondly, we are aware that students may wish to pray during Ramadan and we would like to remind you that we do have a room available for prayer. If your daughter is unsure of the location, she should visit Learning Support and ask for assistance. This room is also available for any students who would like to rest quietly during break or lunchtime if they feel this would be helpful.

As parents, if there are school events that you are unable to attend or are inconvenient during the month, please contact your daughter's Head of Year who will ensure the appropriate people are aware. If it is possible to rearrange or make a personal arrangement, we will do so. Alternatively, if it is not an urgent matter, we will be able to arrange a time following Ramadan.

We know that, on occasion, it might be necessary for health reasons that a student feels they need to break their fast. We appreciate that this could be a source of anxiety for some students and we are aware that this would need to be treated with sensitivity. If your daughter feels they are in this position, they should either go to Pupil Services or speak to their Head of Year/Student Manager who will ensure they get the necessary support.

Finally, we would like to remind parents that, in line with national guidelines, the school policy is to authorise one day of absence for religious observance for

Eid al-Fitr. It is anticipated that this
will fall on 2nd–3rd May this year and, as with any absence from school,
please get in touch with your daughter's Head of Year or tutor if your daughter
is going to be absent.

The school canteen will be organising an Eid menu for early May – please look
out for more details nearer the time in the school bulletin.

Please do get in touch should you have any queries and, even if you do not
anticipate your daughter needing any additional support, please do not
hesitate to let the school know she is fasting if you feel this may be helpful for
us to know.

We would like to take this opportunity to wish you "Ramadan Kareem" and
share our very best wishes for Eid when the times comes.

Mrs George Littler, Headteacher, Didcot Girls' School

It is so important to assure our families that we are not just aware of their backgrounds and cultures but have a deep regard for them. As schools, it is not enough to be aware and make concessions; we must be proactive and agile.

In a similar vein, we celebrate festivals such as Diwali which means a lot to our Hindu students but is certainly enjoyed by the entire school community too. In the week building up to Diwali, we hold 'diya' (lantern) making workshops, where students from across the year groups come together to an event hosted by all hinder students and spend a glorious and leisurely hour painting little clay lamps. These are them formed into a beautiful display to be enjoyed for months to come. We talk to our students about Diwali and the background behind it, the way to celebrate, the foods enjoyed at this time of year, and give some insight into what this festival means to our Hindu students. The catering team always offers an indulgent and thoughtfully planned lunch menu to match the theme of the festival.

The entire school community always looks forward to the first week of February which is when we celebrate Chinese New Year (CNY). Our heritage Chinese students get involved with the planning of events, and every year, I find myself learning something new and exciting about a culture that I know little about. Below is an example of a programme of events put together by one of our Mandarin teachers, Phil Mahoney. Phil's vision and organisation for this celebration means that not only will a Chinese heritage student feel valued by the school community, but hundreds of other students will also experience the opportunity to learn more about an unfamiliar culture.

The list of what we can and should be doing for equality, diversity, and inclusion is long and does not stop here, but in the interest of time an expediency, I will.

Year of the Rabbit – Chinese New Year

Programme of Events 2023

Competition to design poster for Chinese New Year Celebration Week – briefing and set online as optional homework.
Co-write and prepare video for ethos sessions during Chinese New Year celebration week. Focusing on why CNY is important to them and how they celebrate: food, festivals, hometown traditions.
Inter-house poster competition launch. Cascade share to tutors through ethos sessions. 5HP for entering, 20HP for top five entries, and prize for winner.
Deadline for Y7 and Y8 MEP (Mandarin Excellence Programme) poster competition. Y10 and Y11 MEP student reps invited to judge entries
Deadline for inter-house poster competition. All posters must be submitted with name, tutor group, and house to Room 7. Judged by Y10 and Y11 MEP Student reps.
Video by Mandarin Heritage group and shared to tutor groups during ethos sessions
Wonders of the World club – making origami
Lantern making workshop
Calligraphy workshop
Chinese-inspired lunch

Human beings are innately curious, and as schools, we are best placed to both encourage and satiate this curiosity. If we want young people to be respectful, inclusive, and excited about what might feel unfamiliar, we must first enable them to become comfortable with what feels unfamiliar. EDI is the labour of love; it must be driven by passion, empathy, humility, and consistency. In situations where we are starting from scratch, we must be highly intentional in the way we deliver on EDI.

Tool kit

- Ensure that the school community know why EDI is so vital and be aware of the different types of diversities

- Be consistent in the way diversity is marked and celebrated through the school calendar

- Consider having a focus group from the staff and student body to steer any work on EDI further and to hold each other accountable

- Appoint a balanced, diverse, and inclusive student leadership team

House systems

Competition, connection, community

Read on to: explore how school house systems can be used to champion wholesome competition, grow a strong sense of community, and contribute to the overall ethos of our schools. This chapter offers a host of ideas for events, competitions, and activities that can be easily integrated into the school calendar.

School house systems made a resurgence in people's minds after the *Harry Potter* series of books, magicking up images of mysterious wizards and sorting hats. I work with students every day who would do anything to belong to the bewitching cliques of Gryffindor, Ravenclaw, Hufflepuff, and Slytherin: human beings have been evolved to want to belong. This is where a robust and active house system can prove invaluable to our schools' ethos. Granted, school houses continue to be seen largely as the domain of independent boarding schools, but we can see they are beginning to gain popularity in the state sector now too. Identity is at the heart of houses and as Hannah Johnston, Head of Houses at WHS, explains "the initial ties of camaraderie and identity are being formed" as soon as students step into their houses. Belonging to a house is a rite of passage – a passport of sorts if you like (Johnston, 2020).

About a decade ago, the house system at our school existed – but did not do much more than that. All students who came to us in Year 7 joined a house straight away, collected house points, and some partook in any ad hoc house competitions we ran. House assemblies were held termly but felt dry and mundane; house captains had impressive ties and badges but again, not much more. Something had to change in a wholesale way if the house system was ever going to contribute meaningfully to the ethos of the school.

When we decided that we were ready to give our house system a significant rehaul, we began by calling it something memorable: this is how the title *House*

DOI: 10.4324/9781003275985-4

Championships came to be. Further steps included making the houses more visible around the site, stocking up on praise postcards in house colours, investing in beautiful flags on the school site, revamping house assemblies, building significant house competitions into the calendar, and appointing heads of house.

The House Championships are now a real strength at the Trust, bringing a whole host of benefits to our school community. Designed to work vertically (each house has pupils from every year group), they offer a sense of belonging that transcends age, giving our students an opportunity to get to know a range of people outside their lessons and friendship groups. When students join us in Year 7, they are assigned a house which they remain in until they leave in Year 11, offering them continuity in their time with us. Our houses are named after famous women who our young people learn about, look up to, and take a whole lot of inspiration from. The House system allows us to find ways that students and staff can feel more connected to their community; as all staff members belong to a house, the championships provide a unique opportunity for adults and young people to connect outside the classroom. The spirit of competition that is so integral to the house system ensures healthy rivalry for all year groups. The House Championships also play an integral role in promoting our school values both in and outside lessons. Through the system, we reward and recognise the consistent high-level achievements of pupils in their academic work, sporting achievement, of other, less tangible, but equally valuable leadership skills and transferable skills such as teamwork, commitment, and dedication, which are built up in our pupils' time at school. Happily, a robust house system also generates a myriad of opportunities for student leadership which I explain a little later on.

Heads of House

Each house is led and managed by a Head of House. These members of staff – a combination of teaching and non-teaching – meet the House Captain Team regularly to plan events and look closely at what is coming up in the term ahead. They deliver house assemblies together, which is one of the most vital aspects of their role. Their moral purpose is strong and their ability to inspire impressive; they spend a lot of time thinking of creative ways to engage the entire student body and approach their role with our most disadvantaged students at the heart of their thinking. House systems give us a wonderful opportunity for inclusion across the school, in a competitive yet relaxed and low stakes environment. Heads of House must strike the balance between warmth and discipline as while values remain integral, some boundaries can be more relaxed. I have seen Heads of House form some rather special relationships with members of their house, strong and united in their vision for their house through the course of their secondary school journey.

Expectations from Heads of House

- Prepare and support the House Captain Teams in the effective delivery of House assemblies

- Build a collective sense of enthusiasm and healthy competition around the House Championship across all year groups

- Be an active and motivational presence in house events (e.g. the House Opening Ceremony and House Public Speaking Competition)

- Meet termly with the Head of Ethos and other Heads of House to share good practice and plan for upcoming House events

- Meet termly with the House Captain Team to review House Championship progress and plan for continuation and improvement as necessary

- Plan and deliver one House Competition in collaboration with the Director and Head of Ethos

- Write one 'Thought for the Term' each year

- Keep staff updated on forthcoming events and competitions

- Reinforce the inspirational qualities of the House namesake (if these are what your school happen to have!)

I want to spend some time detailing the sorts of additions we made to our calendar when we gave our house system the facelift I mentioned earlier. While these are carefully planned to fit within the culture of our school, they are versatile and adaptable enough to be used in other settings. They should make for good food for thought and inspiration, should you find yourself thinking your house system could benefit from some rebranding.

House Opening Ceremony

The House Opening Ceremony is held every September, at the start of the school year, on the school field. We tend to hold it over lunchtime in the beautiful autumnal sunshine (with a robust Plan B should we be met with autumnal rain instead!) The school field turns into a myriad of colours, banners, costumes, painted faces, and very excited students. Students have the opportunity beforehand, in the weeks that build up to it, to make banners and design mascots for their houses. It is a most joyous break from the routine of school life and is especially powerful in making the new Year 7s feel welcome and settle in. The School Council are out in force selling treats and the PE department organise a host of games around the school site. What is most special about the House Opening Ceremony is the traditional parade led by House Captains and Heads of House around the field, with students as flag bearers followed by fellow house members, cheering with all their might. The parade signals the opening of 'the games' for the rest of the school year. It is organised chaos at its best!

Note: staff duty allocations and patrol need to be carefully considered before-hand, to prevent any disruption or behavioural concerns. In my experience, the students have been too happy and engaged to be disruptive but anyone who works in a school knows we do not take such things for granted!

The House Shout

The 'House Shout' is a most spectacular way to bring students together and has been masterminded by our Music expert, Harriet Edwards. Each house has the stage for ten minutes, which includes entries, exists, and the positioning of individuals. The order of the houses' performance is decided by a member of staff (usually the Head of Music), who takes names out of a hat in public. Followed by this is a most heart-warming afternoon of choral singing, which the students will have been re-hearsing in their houses for the better part of a term. A set of three judges keep notes through the performances, and while they are listening for musicality, house spirit and cohesion are just as important when choosing a winner. The performance pre-sented by each house is student led but relies on the advice and assistance of staff. We try to ensure that members of the Music staff are available for general advice and assistance, but House Captains know that music subject specialists do not play a particular role in any one house's performance unless absolutely unavoidable. We advise that each house should elect a senior student to oversee and coordinate the performance. This person may also like to direct the House Choir. A conductor/ director is advisable too, from within the senior house team. The opportunities for leadership provided by the House Shout are both numerous and eclectic, offering something that will allow every member of the house to feel valued.

We leave it to the houses to decide whether the whole house will perform the song or to arrange the song so that a smaller group sings a verse in harmony. Ac-companiment to songs is permissible, as long as it is in the form of an instrument, such as the piano, being played by a member of the house. Backing tracks are not permissible. The adjudicators award an outright winner and make it clear that the adjudication will include comments on musicality, enthusiasm, the spirit of performance, vitality, conviction; the overriding criteria being 'musicality'. The warmth, community spirit, and joy brought about by the House Shout sustains the morale of the school for weeks to follow and is example of leadership from young people in a most natural and wholesome way.

It is worth noting that while competitions such as the House Shout have tradi-tionally been seen as the preserve of independent schools, there is genuinely no reason that state schools should not initiate such events – they are wholesome and bring joy – what better way to improve the wellbeing of our students? It does not cost anything, all resources – human or otherwise – can be sourced in-house and it is an absolute treat!

Interhouse 'Ted Talk' competition

The interhouse Ted Talk competition is a spin off from the more traditional model of debating competitions. Through the course of the year, our students become familiar with the concept of Ted Talks, having watched some of the exceptionally powerful ones as part of Form Time. For this house competition, students deliver their own Ted Talks to a wide audience of students and staff. The competition is best split into lower and upper school, to keep it fair for participants. Each house appoints a team of speakers beforehand, along with an 'advisory committee'. On the day, these teams are given a topic each and allocated 45 minutes to plan their Ted Talk. The advisory committee assists with the planning, and the team of speakers decide whether who is best fit for delivering the speech on the day. Having a small team instead of one speaker helps to ease the pressure a little, as well as serving the purpose of having back-ups in case of absences or nerves. A range of topics is predetermined by a panel of judges (comprising teaching and non-teaching staff) and are decided bearing in mind the age and interests of students. Teams have access to laptops and phones for any research they deem necessary during their 45 minutes of preparation. Once prepared, all teams have five to seven minutes to present their Ted Talk (the duration can vary depending on the number of houses at the school). The judges work through a range of criteria (delivery, confidence, content, knowledge, engagement with audience, etc.) before announcing the winning three teams at the end and ensuring that celebratory feedback is given to all teams. I have noticed that the skills developed in such a competition are fantastically varied: teamwork, decision making, thinking on your feet, collaborating, collating, and presenting ideas. There is really no limit to the topics available to choose from but to whet your appetites, here are some of my favourites:

- The impact of social media on relationships
- The problem with veganism
- Why should we still read the 'classics'?
- Thoughts – what they really are
- How football saved me
- Why I never eat sugar anymore
- A cup of tea is always, always, the answer.

Interhouse talent show

When it comes to interhouse competitions, talent shows, comedy nights, concerts, and dance-offs are all excellent ideas. At our school, we have traditionally hosted the old-fashioned talent show, which students and families love in equal measure. The fact that both staff and students take part makes this even more exciting. The sorts of talents we have come across range from stand-up comediennes, street dancers, singers and magicians to acrobats, gymnasts, and jugglers. The line-up is exhaustive and never fails to impress! Once the logistics of dates, times, and venue are determined, it is a good idea to establish a project management team. With student leadership at the core of our ethos, I have always found it valuable to hone leadership skills while students are having a brilliant time – the talent show being a top example of such an opportunity. The sorts of roles you can appoint include a

- Team Leader: to keep the vision and the master plan in mind and ensure everyone stays on track

- Talent Leaders: these individuals are responsible for auditions and recruitment of quality talent

- Publicity Leader: to promote the event in a range of ways and organise ticket sales

- Treasurer: to collect and manage money earned through the event

- MC: to compere and present the event and be responsible for keeping the show alive and energetic

- Stage Managers: to ensure that the events run smoothly and in the right order, punctually

- Back-stage Team: to manage stage design, props, costume, makeup, and deal with any situations that arise on the evening

- Front of House Team/League of Friends/School Council: selling tickets, programmes, organising the sale of refreshments, etc.

- Digital Team: to organise music, sound, lighting and to record the event/arrange virtual performances if necessary

Once a strong and reliable team is in place, the next logical step is to consider putting the talent line-up together. For this, departments can be a very good place to start: Art, Music, Drama, and PE are the obvious choices, but it could be well worth it to consult the staff who run clubs too. If there is a lot of interest, auditions will help to taper the list of acts and also ensure an evening of high-quality performances. It's important as well to acknowledge the effort of those who audition but don't make the final cut – house points and letters home are the obvious choice, but a leadership role off-stage may also be appreciated. One of the most entertaining aspects of a talent show is the involvement of staff – whether it is a group performance of 'Dancing Queen' or a (safe) chemical explosion on stage, don't forget to use these acts when promoting ticket sales! In addition to this, posters, flyers, tweets, website announcements, and reminders in form time will all help to promote the show – often there is so much enthusiasm that two shows become necessary. It's a lovely way not just to showcase some incredible talents but also to bring the school community together in an entirely wholesome way.

Interhouse university challenge

This is an excellent opportunity for the Sixth Form to host and run an event – there is no reason why keen members from Year 11 can't take part either! The challenge, as many will know, is one of knowledge, memory, and tenacity, all of which our young people have in abundance. While the television version the series begins with 28 teams, but realistically for an interhouse competition, 7 teams of 3 members each on stage works very well. It's cerebral, heated, and tense: all things fundamental to a successful house system. I particularly love the fact that it invites a range of individuals to get involved in interhouse events. I have worked at schools where interhouse competitions are synonymous with sporting events, leaving many feeling alienated and reluctant. Variety ensures that we are catering for different interests and abilities, across the spectrum.

Interhouse Bake-Off – sort off

I truly have saved the best for the last as I am regularly known to say that if I was not a teacher, I would have been the owner of a cosy little bakery on a street corner which would house everything from cakes and coffee to boardgames and books. However, as this is not a book about cake (watch this space!), let me tell you how cake become an important feature of our school calendar. Every September, to chime with MacMillan's World's Biggest Coffee morning, which raises money for cancer research, we host the Interhouse Bake-Off. I add 'sort off' as a disclaimer since no one bakes on-site. This would be the logistical and health and safety nightmare that few school leaders would willingly walk into. But what a joy our Bake-Off is! After weeks of planning, consulting, and deliberation, our students bring in cakes of an assorted variety (there are no rules here) to represent their house colours. These are displayed through the morning and judged by an eclectic mix of teaching and non-teaching staff, then sliced and sold to collect money for a very worthy cause. Carefully populating the school calendar with an eclectic range of house events keeps all our young people engaged, no matter how varied their interests.

A note on house assemblies

As I mentioned briefly earlier, house assemblies should feel different to regular assemblies. We should be able to let our guard down enough to ensure students look forward to it, but not so much that it results in raucousness. This balance can be tricky to get right and Heads of House are best placed to work along their House team to ensure that structures are in place for this style of assembly. Some aspects of house assemblies must echo that of regular assemblies: promptness of arrival, sensible lining up, entering the hall in an orderly fashion, and respecting 'one voice' – listening when someone else is talking. I also find it useful to plan house assemblies around a theme which allows for a framework, even if it is a fairly forgiving one. With these basic foundations in place, however, we have the opportunity to experiment and get creative. I have seen small group conversations, the use of music as students file in, the use of a 'house' song, brain teasers on power points, whole house vote-taking on upcoming events, drum rolls, cheering, singing, icebreakers, and challenges – it is an exhaustive list. House assemblies should rarely involve just sitting and listening to an authority figure. Rather they should be infused with a strong element of enjoyment and entertainment, celebration, and interaction. In an ideal world, students will walk away from a house assembly feeling energised and buzzing with excitement – especially if the house countdown is kept for the very end! It pays off to go out of our ways to make house assemblies buoyant, memorable, and just that little bit more special.

It certainly pays remarkable dividends to invest in a robust and thriving house system, not only encouraging that all important sense of belonging but also fostering the spirit of healthy competition. Having a house system that is carefully designed, alongside judicious planning for house events, competitions, and assemblies, will ensure that this aspect of school life feeds into a positive and wholesome school community. The suggestions I have provided are by no means exhaustive; house competitions can emerge from any aspect of school life and a wide variety of subjects. Maths departments can host Darts Competitions, Science Departments can organise rocket launching on the fields during Science Week, Modern Foreign Languages could have a 'crepe making' competition, and Film Studies might plan a photography competition in autumn. These ideas, of course, all belong to some of the most passionate colleagues I have known over the years, but my bigger point is that creative licence can go a long way in making our house systems energetic and exciting for our young people.

Tool kit

- Consider rebranding and relaunching your house system if it feels a little tired or lacklustre

- Appoint Heads of House where possible; they will keep the house system alive and energetic

- Populate your calendar with a diverse range of house events, to cater to a host of tastes and interests

- Make house assemblies unique and exciting; loosen the structure just enough to make them feel special

- Keep the houses visible around the school site to promote wholesome competition among the school community

5 The growth mindset in action

Read on to: discover the most powerful ways to use the Growth Mindset theory within the school setting and how to enhance confidence, self-belief, and academic performance by making small changes in our interactions with young people.

This chapter is based on the Growth Mindset theory developed by Dr Carol Dweck, Stanford University psychologist, in 2006. Based on neuroscience, the theory invites us to believe that we can improve our ability, skill, and performance with the right mindset (Dweck, 2017). Investing the time and energy into cultivating a growth mindset in schools can reap phenomenal rewards, both academically and pastorally. The idea of a flexible and pliant mindset gives young people hope and belief that they can and *will* do better, if the right strategies and approach are being put into place. This improves students' response to feedback, increases self-esteem, and enables them to feel empowered about their journeys. While schools are generally very good at illustrating the theory of Growth Mindset, what is more challenging is its day-to-day implementation. This chapter suggests a powerful link between teaching leadership skills and implementing the growth mindset in schools: strategies include meaningful praise and encouragement; catering to a range of leadership styles through carefully developed opportunities; differentiating leadership opportunities both in and outside the classroom (by using tools like the Leadership Ladder – much more detail on this in Chapter 2); and cultivating the values of persistence, hard work, and ambition. The chapter also includes staff and student voice on how the growth mindset works in practice both in and outside the classroom and offers a thorough and strategic approach towards employing it in schools.

When it was introduced and gained popularity, educational institutions around the world were instantly seduced by the Growth Mindset theory. Many schools,

DOI: 10.4324/9781003275985-5

including the ones in our Trust, tend to revisit the theory regularly and they are wise to do so. It is after all a real lifeline for us at schools: it generates evidence-based hope that our abilities, skills, performance, and even our intelligence can all improve with the right mindset and targeted intervention. It invites us to reconsider the way in which we view our mental and emotional resources. Dweck explores the powerful connection between the way we think and the way our education, careers, relationships, and lives unfold. Just this switch in our attitudes and beliefs about our abilities can alter the course of our journeys, she argues. It is a step beyond believing in ourselves; it is an absolute validation in what we are capable off when we change or mindsets and invest the hard work. Both the hard work and the mindset are indispensable for the theory to work. The magic only seems to happen when the two are combined. The research and writing that accompanies the theory has powerfully supported with promoting its essential message. Several books have been written to convey the power of the growth mindset at all levels. Excellent examples include:

I Can't Do That, YET: Growth mindset, by Esther Pia Cordova follows the journey of Enna, a young girl who struggles to look beyond self-doubt and fear and realises through the course of a dream just what she is capable off with dedication, resilience and sheer hard work. Despite the narrative style chosen by Cordova, the story never suggest that the growth mindset is a magical overnight fix. It takes patience and the wisdom that comes from persistence and dedication.

The Cow Tripped Over the Moon, Tony Wilson (Candlewick Press, 2015).

She Persisted: 13 American Women Who Changed the World by Chelsea Clinton & Alexandra Boiger (Philomel Books, 2018).

School leaders are perfectly aware that endorsing and investing in the growth mindset can lead to significant gains: it improves students' response to feedback, increases self-esteem, and enables the school community to feel empowered about their abilities and prospects. It is an invitation to dream and to dream big. So far, so good. I am a long-time committed fan of the Growth Mindset theory. Unfortunately, the believing is the easy bit.

While schools are generally good at extolling and illustrating the virtues of the Growth Mindset theory, what is much more challenging is its day-to-day implementation. I spent years talking about the theory impassionedly on any occasion that presented itself, but always seemed to stop short at the stage where everyone wondered – 'Great! How do we switch our mindsets now?' This seems to be a stumbling block for lots of educators. I had to give this a great deal of thought: who had the switch that one could flick to rest a mindset? Fortunately, I had some luck. Trial and error, fascinating conversations with colleagues, and pressing curiosity mean that I am now equipped with several steps we can take straight away to make the theory of growth mindset spring into action. My hope is that these will help you in the way that they have helped our school community:

Meaningful, individualised, and thoughtful praise

Students can quickly see through a tokenistic compliment. For teachers, this means that we must get creative about the ways in which we word our feedback so that it serves its intended purpose: to encourage our students to take pride in their work and strive for even better. A small first step towards this is to use students' names in their exercise books. An instant connection is made right there. Keeping the praise specific helps: "Zara, I love how unique your nocturnal metaphors are". This will mean much more than: "Great use of language techniques". Praise their methods, strategies, effort, persistence, enjoyment, courage, and the willingness to try. Praise the way they deal with disappointment to bounce back and recover. Don't save the praise just for excellence in achievement – the process is quite often just as important as the result. I have come to recognise the importance of the process in all aspects of life and sincerely wish someone had taken the time to help me understand it when I was younger and obsessed with the end result. I have had to learn to become aware of my processes and perceive the end result as just one component of the journey. How can we possibly expect young people to stay motivated if we place all the importance on a final grade, mark, or report? When we manage to make the journey enjoyable and meaningful, growth automatically takes place. It feels much more natural and organic. My daughter has been taking piano lessons since the age of 8 and is now 14; like most children, she started with no knowledge at all. In these six years, she has sat three grading exams, in the build-up to which she has 'upped her game' a lot. However, it is those bog-standard Wednesday evenings, which she has stayed thoroughly committed to, and those ten minutes a day of practice that have allowed her to play fluently today. The big moments are so rare that they are almost irrelevant. Growth happens organically, over a period of time, when no one is looking. We need to talk to our students about these everyday moments and praise their commitment to persisting when things start feeling tedious and boring. It is the space in which we grow as individuals. It is worth sharing with our students that praise is both a validation of their efforts and achievements but also the invitation to a challenge. Unfortunately, generic and closed phrases of praise can be redundant, counterproductive, and can lose impact quickly.

Communicate home

At the Trust, we use postcards home as one of our main reward currencies and, not surprisingly, we have found that a hand-written note that reaches home does wonders for a young person's self-esteem. In my experience, a few telephone calls home on a Friday afternoon, with the explicit purpose of praising a student's effort, can have amazing results too. It shows that our feedback is in no way lazy, and we have made time to convey it in a meaningful, sincere way. Students appreciate this more than they let on. Communicating home on a regular basis no doubt adds to teachers' ever growing to-do list, but the relationships forged as a result, whereby the school and family work together in the best interest of the student, pays back dividends in plenty. When I communicate home, I share the next step with parents and carers; I let them know when I have changed the goal posts so that they mirror the young person's growth mindset and feel ambitious on their behalf and cheer them on from the seats in the front row.

Make it visual

Posters and visual displays really can go one of two ways, but in my experience, they have a valuable role to play when it comes to the Growth Mindset. A visual representation of the theory has definite 'stickability', especially like the one below, which shows young people how the brain absorbs and adapts to the growth mindset. It speaks to them a lot louder than 'you can do it!' These visuals also serve as subconscious and non-intrusive reminders to students as they go about their business on the school site. For many years, my classroom displayed a wall size display of 'Growth Mindset Language'; essentially, these were words and phrases we could use intentionally to remind ourselves that we have the self-belief needed to succeed. As my ethos duties increased at the Trust, I lost my classroom but always smile when I pass by it and notice my colleague has decided to keep it up, years on. The dual coding of words and images helps with keeping the Growth Mindset narrative alive and steadily drip feeds the messages we want to convey.

Lead by example

I am not convinced that as a community of teachers we spend enough time talking to our students about our own journeys. We are almost always strapped for time, I acknowledge, but those little opportunities, where we can slip in an anecdotal reference about how our own mindsets underwent a change, or how we overcame a mental barrier to achieve a goal, will always have more impact than the explication of a theory. We have evolved to love stories and they are one of the most effective pedagogical tools in my kit. Ultimately, if we want students to engage meaningfully with our messages, we must employ the methods that work best. And storytelling works wonders. I have shared with my students over the years the courage it took me to become comfortable with public speaking; the complete change in self-belief I had to undergo, from crumbling into bits at the prospect of raising my hand in class to flying in a C-130 (it doesn't help that I am scared of flying) to speak at a national debating contest held at an air force base in Pakistan. It took years of self-talk, self-soothing, and practise; I tell my students how initially I felt like a fraud but the more I worked on my public speaking skills, the more authentic my experience felt. It was not so much 'faking' the self-talk as an almost maternal instinct to reassure a child that all will be well, even when you are not sure it will.

My students always listen intently to my stories as it allows them access to a part of me that they know little about. Sharing my experiences, especially my fears and frustrations, is far more empowering than any facades of infallibility I have tried to convey in the past. Recently, our Head of Year 12 asked me to deliver an 'inspirational assembly' to her cohort of 240 + 16- to 17-year olds. That was the only brief – she said I could speak about anything I liked. The freedom of choice was exhilarating. Eventually, I decided to talk about my relationship with anxiety and the mindset I ultimately adopted to improve my situation. There is always going to be a professional balance which we as educators know all too well, but where there is scope to share our growth, we must.

Encourage reflection

Self-reflection has always been integral to personal growth and leadership. It allows us to take a moment regularly to stop and consider, mull over, deconstruct, and investigate what we did, how we did it, and why we did it – would we do it again, and if so, would we do it differently? When put this way, self-reflection sounds like a rather 'grown-up' concept and one that we may not automatically expect from children and teenagers. We should. This time spent pausing and reflecting is not just invaluable in grounding and steading our students but also enables them to track how far they have come and what is needed to reach their destination, as it were. Think of a long and convoluted road trip, involving motorways, country roads, rugged terrain, and unfamiliar surroundings: imagine never stopping to have a break or consulting your map to gather a sense of what is next and how best to get there. Fair enough, a satellite navigation system will pull us through this, so suspend your disbelief and imagine this journey without one! Just the thought of it makes me, for one, anxious and confused. Self-reflection is a time to get our bearings and renew our motivation on any journey, literal or metaphorical. I have discovered that the best way to ensure we teach this to our students in an inclusive way is through journalling. I discovered journalling as a form of regular classroom practice in Los Angeles, America, where I attended a conference on girls' education. Classroom teachers spoke passionately about how journalling their progress in the last few minutes of the lesson had proved priceless in the progress their students were making. The very act of being aware of the process, without doing much else, was reaping powerful rewards. I heard from a Mathematics teacher who had been trialling journalling in his Maths classes and reported that students were becoming much more conscious of how far they had come, as opposed to just frustrated by everything they couldn't yet do. I brought this strategy back to the UK with me and experimented with it almost immediately. That year my Year 11 exam class, mostly comprised of struggling students (many of whom were unlikely to pass without serious intervention), had exceptionally low levels of motivation. They seldom felt like they were making any progress and had lost faith in their own abilities. I decided to buy them all some lovely journals (they were a small group, and I was keen to experiment) and off we went. The last eight minutes of every English lesson were spent journalling any and everything: how the lesson had gone, how they felt about the subject, what they understood on the day, how they might improve, their frustrations, their victories – there were no limits! The pages began filling up quickly and many asked to take their journals home. Very slowly, I noticed some of their confidence growing as they began to visually track how far they had come. They could turn back, literally, and be reminded of what they can achieve. I never had to use the term Growth Mindset with them because it was not necessary – they were acting on its core principles which is what mattered. Becoming aware of the learning and cognitive process was building their sense of control. Being reflective about their journey was keeping them on track and proving cathartic at the same time, and their grades were reflecting this mindset shift. Meditation gurus and spiritual leaders will tell us that to be aware is everything; I have found enormous benefits in teaching young people about self-awareness and reflection as they journey through school life.

Normalise failure

As schools, we are beginning to realise that we need to remove the stigma around the words 'failing' and 'failure'. Part of having a growth mindset is acknowledging, accepting, and unpacking failure in order to grow from it. Viewed this way, failure becomes an opportunity to develop, and I would even say that I welcome it from time to time. I have found that sharing experiences of failure is as powerful as sharing stories of success. Unfortunately, the obsession with perfection and getting it right all the time (no doubt exacerbated by public examination pressures) does not ultimately serve the purpose of letting people improve and grow. Teachers worldwide will testify that many students can become so fearful of getting it wrong that the anxiety around "failure" often prevents them from trying in the first place. At the Trust, we endeavour to talk about failure openly and honestly, enabling our young people to realise that it is a shared universal experience that need not hold them back.

Welcoming a good challenge

As teachers, we are perfectly placed to role-model how exciting and gratifying a challenge can feel. We grow as a result of embracing challenges, both academic and emotional, but this is not necessarily how every young person will view a difficult test question. Model your thought processes when you encounter a challenging question – talk them through your approach and be as open as possible. This is the sort of connection students really love. Allow students to see that challenges can feel difficult yet rewarding. The over emphasis on crispness and slickness can sometimes alienate students and work against us. The reality is that learning is sometimes messy. The human mind is accustomed to fear tests of any kind and changing mindset here can change the game completely. When my student leaders prepare to make speeches to large crowds, I invite them to visualise being successful and view their nervousness as excitement instead of dread. The good news is that our brains are very responsive to such persuasion and our performance when tackling a challenge of any sort will be vastly improved as a result. As part of this, of course, it is important to teach and model risk-taking; our students will benefit by learning how to weigh out the consequences, plan ahead, watch out for their own fears and anxieties. Armed with this knowledge, the growth mindset can be particularly effective as we are giving students more autonomy over their learning process and validating their individual approach to risks and challenge. Exams and results can make the strongest of us wary and uncomfortable, but a change in psyche alongside carefully modelled risk-taking can help to overcome these obstacles and let our students experience the success they want. It is transformational to remind young people that our beliefs about ourselves have the power to transform our thinking, our actions, and our lives.

Dismantle the myth that growth mindset is magic

Here is where we stand to lose a lot of buy-in from young people. It is important to convey that the growth mindset leads to incremental, yet significant gains. When these accumulate, the overall picture looks phenomenal – it is a marathon, not a sprint, but happily, the rewards come along the way and not just at the end. Progress is rarely linear or quick, nor will we suddenly be achieving the unthinkable. However, the magic comes from how our fundamental beliefs about ourselves can change our entire life's course. It comes from realising that when we believe that our intelligence and abilities are fixed or determined, we develop an unhealthy obsession with proving ourselves rather than believing that we have the capacity to keep growing. Dweck has addressed this misconception in the latest and most up-to-date edition of her book In order to convey this to students that we need to become more cognisant of the incremental gains and progress, not just in results but also in attitude, revision, preparation, commitment. It is important to encourage students to look back and become more conscious of progress and begin to track just how far they have come both in terms of skills and abilities; it is less helpful to sell them a dream promising the stars and the moon.

Don't always glorify hard work

I have had to train myself out of insisting to students that all learning is enjoyable: this may sound a somewhat counterintuitive, but sometimes, it is important to come clean with students about hard work being, well, hard! I confess to my students when I find some aspect of the topic heavy or dull and I acknowledge there are times when revision can feel onerous. Equally, the rewards of consistent hard work and sincere efforts more than makes up for the process. Validating students' experience both when they are enjoying lessons and when they are not does ultimately make it easier to get them on board. Keep an eye on the result, and yes, enjoy the process but don't expect it to feel rewarding at each stage. Furthermore, I believe students benefit a great deal when we distinguish "working hard" from "working smart". My nine years of teaching at a girls' school has presented numerous examples of students working much harder than they needed to. The reminder (with modelling) that efficient, smart, and flexible ways of working can be just as effective if not more so is an important one. The sooner we teach young people to organise, prioritise, and multi-task the better.

From a personal perspective, the growth mindset has been invaluable in a much wider sense too, extending far beyond the academic world. It allows me to acknowledge that I have the ability to keep learning, growing, and evolving as a mother, as a teacher, and as an individual. The idea that my personal growth is boundless and infinite makes me excited and immensely curious about myself. The growth mindset allows me, if I may quote Einstein, "to comprehend a little of this mystery each day". Can you imagine the rewards we can reap in schools if we create clear and strong pathways for our young people to understand and employ their growth mindsets?

Tool kit

- Take time to dismantle the myths around the growth mindset; ensure that students understand what it really means

- Thoughtful, tailored praise for students

- Visual displays of the Growth Mindset theory around school

- Encourage young people to have a vision and keep revisiting it

- Teach students to track and acknowledge any progress

- Invite students to welcome a challenge

- Talk openly about failure

- Delineate working hard and working smart

- See your challenges as opportunities...
- Reflect each day on what you've failed at (and learned from)...
- Stop seeking approval from others
- Identify opportunities to celebrate the success of others...
- Focus on rewarding actions, not traits...
- Start using the word "yet" more often

Complicating failure

Read on: Discover how we can talk to our students about failure in a wholesome and enabling way while teaching them about leadership. Learn how to help young people understand that schools provide the safe setting to take risks, fail, learn, and rebuild. This chapter shows why shying away from failure is ultimately a flawed investment in our young people.

"What if?" to "So what?"

In the summer of 2022, after being struck by Covid-19 for the second time and having become all too aware of how much the virus had depleted my energy supplies, I decided I would take concerted steps to rebuild myself. I was by this time also living with crippling generalised anxiety which had been exacerbated by the pandemic. Home had become my safe place and I was relieved not to have to leave it much. Knowing full well I needed to do something concrete to get back to 'normality', I decided I would start running. Five or so years ago, I had been a regular runner and could go 40 minutes or so without stopping. If you are reading this as an athlete or marathon runner, you will no doubt be less impressed than someone who, like me, runs mainly when there is danger! I made a running schedule, reactivated my smart watch, bought a running bottle, and a forehead flashlight – this is how optimistic I was feeling. Saturday morning arrived and it was time for Run 1. The heavens opened and I undid the laces on my running shoes, slipping back into weekend gear. I would go the next morning, I assured myself. The next morning, I woke up with the hangover that perhaps only the parents of toddlers will appreciate. I had been up several times in the night soothing an unsettled toddler with a badly blocked nose. This time, I did not even attempt to put the running shoes on. It would just have to wait. As the week passed, I thought about Run 1 every day and even when the skies were clear and no other barriers presented, my brain managed to find an excuse. Some evenings I got myself fully ready and at the last minute decided to do a 'home' work-out instead; I was still burning calories and building muscle I told myself, but in the reassuring comfort of my home. This continued for weeks before a good friend decided to intervene with brutal honesty: "you are scared to leave the front door aren't you, Gohar?" he said. "You are scared you will go out, clam up, fail to complete the run, and come home. You don't want to step out, so you don't have to feel like a failure afterwards". It was the truth; I was petrified of failing at something I did well enough in the past. And the fear of that feeling, it turns out, was the only barrier there ever was. To think that in this case the stakes were low – no college or university admissions depended on my ability to run, nor did I have to worry about letting my family down. I was genuinely just worried about how I would cope with my own feelings of failing at something relatively innocuous. Imagine then, what an anxious 16-year old might feel about public examinations, a college interview, or indeed applying for a leadership role at school. The truth is that the dread of failure puts us on the backfoot from the very start. We go into challenging situations with our most prominent thought being 'What if?'. The same brutally honest friend suggested something deceptively simple, that I believe has changed my life: he said, swap 'what if?' with 'so what?'. So what if I ran for a minute and felt completely out of breath? I could take as long a break as I needed. So what if I was spotted by old running friends who shot me a look of pity? They would forget in a few minutes and so would I. So what if I had a panic attack? I would stop until it passed like it always does, and I could carry on or walk back home. I went for a run that evening. And because I had ready responses to all the 'what if' questions my brain presented, my mind decided the game was not as enjoyable anymore and I had a glorious 30 minutes in the beautiful outdoors. What if the anxiety returned tomorrow? Well, so what?

Talking to young leaders about failing

I promise not to refer to my running again in this book but the important lesson it taught me was that when the sheer thought of failure begins to cripple us, it is time to get more comfortable in its presence. Even if you don't befriend it (let's be real – no one ever really wants to fail), begin to accept and tolerate it. What we resist persists. This lesson is one that I now routinely share with our students when exploring leadership: avoiding failure or conversations about it will not make it go away. If only it were that easy!

Let's take these musings into a school setting. No discussion on successful leadership is ever truly complete without a healthy dose of conversation based around failure. It has taken me three decades to learn just how critical it is to talk about failure openly and often, especially in schools where we deal with hundreds of young people every day, all of whom will experience feelings of failure, and the vast majority will have little idea how to process these feelings. While we have seen the world evolve and progress in ways unimaginable to us in the past (we had entire schooling systems running without anyone leaving their homes during months of lockdown!), there seem to remain some fundamental aspects of life where we seem to have made very little advancement: one of these is the way in which we talk (or not as the case may be) about vulnerability and failure. Failure largely continues to be a topic of embarrassment or disgrace, left well alone in public, and a cause for distress in private lives. When we come across famous writers, celebrities, sporting legends, or world leaders talk openly about failure, it is with the advantage of hindsight; their stories of failure generally tend to get much better as they divulge how they overcame obstacles and broke down barriers to become who they are today. These stories are often told from a place of accomplishment and success, with a hint of the 'happily ever after', though I grant they are not always as reductive as that. So, who is telling the stories of failure without exoticising or glamorising the narrative? The trouble is that not very many people are. In order to taste success, our young people need us to complicate traditional tropes of failure. Honest, sincere, and open conversations about failure are integral to the ethos of a school. If my 15 years of secondary teaching experience has shown me one thing, it is just how much the fear of failure holds young people back from so much as taking a first step. The lack of open and honest conversations about failure as a shared universal experience is dangerously counterproductive. In recent years, I have devoted much time to develop strategies for building and sustaining openness about failure within the safety of the school setting and demonstrate how this leads to creativity, confidence, and a risk-taking mindset in our young people. Schools have a lot of work to do to create a climate where feelings of failure are normalised in order to make goal setting, creative problem solving, and risk-taking more exciting and appealing. Of course, if we are going to get used to talking about failure, we must befriend its close companion, vulnerability.

Vulnerability

To me, no one in our times writes or speaks about vulnerability better than Brene Brown. Brown insists that our capacity to be emotionally or mentally injured and to be willing not to camouflage it has the power to change lives. When we are 'not okay', we are just that: 'not okay'. We do ourselves no favours by pretending we are okay when we are not. Yes, we may manage to delude those around us into believing all is well and we are perfectly in control of our emotions, but there is no deluding ourselves. When entire societies avoid being seen as vulnerable, often going a step beyond this by negating feelings of vulnerability, we create communities that are built on false and dangerous foundations. We know that when these foundations ultimately give way under overwhelm or distress, the results will be catastrophic and the mess truly unpleasant. This notion of 'I am absolutely fine', 'you are absolutely fine' and the assumption that it would be unacceptable to be anything but 'okay' and 'fine' is little better than an entire village applauding the emperor's new clothes. When someone is struggling but will not show it, and we won't see it, leave alone talk about it, we become willing participants in this mass project of ignorance and denial.

Vulnerability and masculinity in an all-boys' setting

Let's focus for a moment on how vulnerability relates in particular to the experience of young boys in our secondary schools. As educators, we know boys are struggling daily with the fear of appearing vulnerable against the tide of toxic masculinity, which, sadly, is not as much a thing of the past as we would like it to be. Working at the only all-boys' state school in Oxfordshire means that conversations about masculinity, including toxic versions of it, are always on the table. I have spent a great deal of time unpicking the sorts of fears that make our boys so unwilling to talk about their vulnerabilities. It will perhaps come as no surprise that most boys in our schools remain unwilling to share their feelings, are obsessed with appearing strong and infallible, and prefer to bottle up fears and anxieties. And who can blame them? This is precisely what life has taught our boys to do over hundreds of years. Men may no longer all be hunter gatherers anymore but the toxic expectation to remain strong no matter what, remains.

As educators, we strive for change and at the boys' school, we work to nurture an environment that enables all our young boys to feel vulnerable, empowered, authentic, valued, and most important of all – happy. Despite a great deal of research and several significant endeavours to repair the damage caused by the tropes of toxic masculinity, it prevails and continues to cause harm. The pressures on boys to fit into an archaic framework of masculinity are immense. In schools, we need to work actively and strategically to cultivate a culture that allows boys to thrive; where there is support and space for boys to explore their thoughts and feelings openly and freely. Our aim is to enable all our young people to grow, while building the values of leadership, resilience, compassion, and confidence. Such an ethos needs to grow organically and takes time to embed but here are five tried and tested ideas that can be embedded straight away to begin to cultivate a culture for modern masculinity:

1 Ensure that all our students develop an authentic understanding of what toxic masculinity is: to dismantle this culture, young people need to recognise it first. In schools, we can find a range of platforms to convey this, including tutor time, assemblies, guest speakers, and judiciously crafted reading lists. Find an engaging way to convey to students that toxic masculinity is a set of undesirable traits that are traditionally associated with being male. These can include physical or emotional domination, aggressive or violent behaviour, a tough exterior, the need to be infallible, the urge to be in control, an immunity to danger, vulnerability, and fear.

2 Encourage a widening of the conversational scope: most boys are socially conditioned to restrict themselves to a frustratingly limited scope of conversation. Very broadly speaking, these can include sport, gaming, films, music but steering well clear of anything more emotional or 'deep'. There will always be some welcome exceptions to this general conditioning. At schools, we can create opportunities for thoughtful face-to-face discussions and tutor time or assemblies are ideal opportunities to do this. A predesigned range of topics for discussion, which can then be opened for discussion in a supportive environment. Include anything from theatre and politics to philosophy and food – whet their appetite for topics they may not have explored before.

3 Revisit the curriculum to represent wholesome and nuanced masculinity: schools are generally better at promoting female inspirational role models than male. Subject specialists should be thinking carefully about exposing young people to an eclectic range of male role models who embody a diversity of traits and strengths.

4 Dismantle the shame in vulnerability: toxic masculinity correlates vulnerability with feelings of shame and failure. At schools, we have a responsibility to 'normalise' feelings of failure and vulnerability which are perfectly common human experiences. It is empowering for students to recognise that teachers and leaders all make mistakes and what matters is how we respond to these mistakes. What can we do? Talk openly about failure – be clear about strategies for recovering from failure. It is just as important to talk about failure as success.

5 Make feminism inclusive: it is short-sighted and alienating to make 'equality' and 'feminism' areas exclusive to female students. It is important that we make our male students an integral part of promoting equality and exploring feminism. Boys' active participation in gender justice and equality amongst the sexes will strengthen individuals and societies. Boys and men play an incredibly important role in challenging others over sexism, misogyny, and violence so we need to make feminism all-inclusive territory. Try celebrating 'International Women's Day' with real aplomb at your all-boys' school for a positive start.

Being vulnerable in front of our students, within reason of course – we are all sensible and know our limits – is important so we can role model the way in which we cope with feelings of failure. There is little point in presenting ourselves as emotionally watertight when we know this is inaccurate. It is much more about teaching our students that vulnerability and failure are normal, healthy pitstops on the route to success, not barriers. It is about allowing our students to shift the obsession with perfection and focus on learning and self-growth, which is far from linear – and far from perfect.

In her essay 'Vulnerability in the Classroom', LynnAnne Lowrie suggests that even our practical pedagogical approaches, such as 'hiding behind the podium' can 'can set us up for impersonal and distant relationships'. Lowrie even says that technology (we call it Death by Power Point) "draws attention toward content and away from ourselves" (Lowrie, 2019). A whole host of things that we sometimes subconsciously do, can make us that little bit less 'real' to students. In recent years, I have spent a lot of time modelling 'live' essays to students, spelling mistakes and grammatical errors and all, giving myself time to check, re-write, etc. Students prefer this much more to the times when I hand them a flawlessly written model answer; the messiness is part of the process, and the vulnerability can lead to an empowering empathy. When I was new to the teaching profession, the situations I dreaded most in the classroom were those in which I had to say, "I don't know" or hastily move on to a different topic of conversation to avoid the embarrassment off somehow letting myself and my students down. It has taken several years, extensive reading around failure and vulnerability and many conversations with colleagues and mentors much wiser than me, to be able to welcome a situation in the classroom when I don't know the answer and discover it along with my students. This also offers me the opportunity to thank a student for making me think hard about something or piquing my curiosity. It allows me to convey to them that I too am learning every day. One of my ex-colleagues, who also happens to be the most wonderful teaching assistant I have ever known, would say to students several times a day that "every day is a school day". She openly and proudly shared her fascination with how much young people had to teach her, how she became a teaching assistant despite her struggles with dyslexia and how much empathy she had with anyone who experienced learning difficulties. In the eight years that I worked with Mandy Jones, the thing that struck me most was how students connected with her; they saw her as "real" and very human, and it became a standing joke in the English department that students were only ever really looking for Mrs. Jones! Normalising feelings of failure and vulnerability does not happen overnight. Nor is there a magic formula or workshop that we can attend to get us feeling comfortable with failure. It requires a culture shift, and open and honest conversations amongst staff on students is the best place to start. Being open to feelings of vulnerability consistently overtime would lead the entire school community to recognise and appreciate that "this is how we do things here". A few years ago, sensing quite heavily that we were all shying away from talking or even thinking about failure I chose failure to be our thought for the term. It felt like a brave choice given that it was unusual compared to our regular fare: resilience, responsibility, kindness, and compassion. But it also felt honest and right. I made a plea to the staff community to see if anyone would come forward to contribute to a portfolio of written pieces that went on to be called *The Chronicles of Failure*. Clearly, I was not the only one who sensed the need for enabling conversations around vulnerability as I had colleagues volunteering within minutes of my e-mail being sent out. That term we used the words failure and vulnerability more than we've done in years as a school community and discovered what a disservice we do to each other by pretending these concepts don't exist.

In the rest of this chapter, you can enjoy a selection of these contributions to *The Chronicles of Failure*.

Mr Dingley (Head of Music)

Mediocrity was viewed as failure when I was at school – if you weren't at the top of the cohort for a particular subject/sport/activity, this meant you 'couldn't' do it and there was no point trying to improve. This culture of singular success only if you were at the top was toxic and many of my friends gave up in numerous subjects, achieving, eventually, unacceptably low results in their GCSEs. To combat this ethos, students at my school found a niche where they excelled and celebrated this, and for me, this niche was always Music, in particular, playing the piano.

As a result, I pushed my way through The Associated Board of the Royal Schools of Music (ABRSM) grade system, always needing to have the highest grade to maintain my status. I usually scraped through, achieving passes and merits if I was really lucky.

However, when I reached Grade 8, my luck ran out – I did not receive enough marks to pass; I failed. Having got my results, my teacher and those around me put my failure down to a harsh examiner as there was no way I could have failed because I was so good at the piano.

Disgruntled, I learned a new set of pieces and entered myself for a retake. I practised and felt ready to take the exam again. I left the exam feeling successful; however, a few weeks later, the letter arrived to say that, once again, I had not achieved a pass mark; I had failed once again. Once again, the blame lay with the exam board – it was their fault for not seeing how amazing I was at the piano. Underneath the façade, this was a critical blow for my image as an excellent pianist. I considered giving up and not bothering with Grade 8 – I didn't need it.

I did give up – I stopped piano lessons. I could still play well; I didn't need Grade 8 to be the best pianist in the school. I considered dropping A-level Music as I wanted to study medicine at university, and I didn't need it – I didn't want to be part of something where I was deemed a failure.

A few weeks later, a conversation with the accompanist at choir rehearsal resulted in me having a trial piano lesson with her. She listened to me play and her feedback was devastating: my technique was terrible, my rhythm all over the place and I was not consistent or coherent. She noted that it was unsurprising that I had failed Grade 8 twice when I was not good enough to even be entered. Her words almost brought me to tears; however, I persevered with her. This was the first time in my musical life that anyone had told me that I needed to improve and **how** I should do it. It was the **how** that made the difference to my mindset.

This new teacher took me back to the beginning and started again; she showed me what I was doing wrong and how to make it better. She shredded everything

I knew about playing and gave me exercise after exercise to build up my technique and understanding of how the piano should be played. She developed my control and my musicianship, and further taught me how to practise properly – something which I had never done well. This teacher showed me that I could be the player I aspired to be if I practised effectively and regularly.

A year later, I retook my Grade 8 and passed (with a good merit) and am a better musician and person for it – not because of the qualification itself, but because of what I had to put myself through to get it. I came to the realisation that I did not have to be the best to be successful; indeed, it was never going to be possible to be the best at everything but that should not stop me from enjoying learning, practising, and playing.

Miss Stella Vassiliou (teacher of English and professional tutor)

In the summer between the end of my university degree and starting my first teaching job, I had two main tasks: (1) Find somewhere to live; (2) Learn to drive. I was 21 years old, and the world lay at my feet. I was both exhilarated and terrified.

Having grown up in London, I had never previously had any reason to drive. The transport systems are so good where I lived (near Wembley) that I used to get everywhere that I needed to go by bus, tube, or on foot. But now that I was moving to Oxfordshire, a car was going to become a necessity.

Step 1 was the theory test. I knew that I could do exams – I had had a lot of practice! – so I approached it in the same way as any previous test. I studied hard, prepared well, and got 100%. Job done.

When it came to the practical, things were rather less certain. Although I didn't realise it at the time, I didn't have a very good teacher. My progress was slow and when he suggested that I take my test at the end of the summer, I knew that I wasn't ready. But I thought that, probably, everyone must feel like this about their driving test. After all, I was being asked to be solely responsible for a complex piece of machinery that could be lethal: I was bound to be nervous.

The morning came and my mum and dad sent me off with great confidence. They believed in me; I had worked hard; it would be fine.

But it wasn't fine. I absolutely and entirely and dismally and without any doubt about it failed. What made it worse was that the examiner had laughed at me. When I had completed the parallel park part of the test, he exclaimed, "You could drive a motorbike between you and the kerb!" The aim had been to get as close to the kerb as possible.

When I failed that first driving test, I was absolutely devastated. I had literally never failed at anything before. I can remember sobbing my heart out when I got back home to my mum and dad's, feeling embarrassed, humiliated, and stupid. I never wanted to get back into a car again.

It was not until I was living in Oxfordshire that I was brave enough to try again. A new teacher, a new start. The first instructor I had after this said to me dismissively, as I got into the car, "You've been taught by a man, haven't you?! You don't need a cushion to sit on!" and I spent the rest of the lesson desperately trying to peer over the steering wheel to see at least some of the road! Thankfully, the second driving school I tried was better.

By March of my first year of teaching, I felt ready to have another go at the test. I had perfected my manoeuvres, was able to change gears smoothly, and felt more comfortable driving on dual carriageways. But I still wasn't sure that I'd pass.

I didn't. I made too many minor faults and just missed out.

The worse thing about this second failure was the reaction of my best friend. I remember telling her on the phone: "I failed again." Her response, "Ha! Are you joking?!" was not particularly kind or helpful. The tears came again but less overwhelmingly than before.

Eventually, I did pass my driving test at the third attempt. I did it just four weeks after my failed second test, drove the same route, and made just two minor faults. Basically, a perfect drive. I've rarely felt prouder than I did driving home in my instructor's car on that day.

I have absolutely no doubt that I am a much better driver, as a result of having to do three tests, than I would have been otherwise. I am also much more empathetic than I might have been otherwise to the failures of others, especially my friends. Failing was horrible: I didn't enjoy it, but I am grateful for what it taught me. I know I can fail and that the world does not end. I know that I can be resilient. And I know that I'm now a very, very good driver.

Mr Chris Fulwell (Teacher of Mathematics and Head of Year)

Hello. My name is Mr Fulwell and I have been a failure many times in my life. I'd like to share two different types of failures in my life and how they've really, really helped me.

A long time ago, before I became a Maths Teacher, I wanted to be an actor (this will be a shock, I know, as I'm a shy, quiet person) and I decided to apply to Drama School. Drama schools teach you how to act in lots of different ways, you get to work on your voice, rehearse and perform lots of different plays, do some stage fighting, do a lot of exercise, and even do some singing… Applying to Drama School is a bit like applying to university except rather than having your academic qualifications looked at and then working really hard for some exams, you have to prepare some speeches from plays and then perform these speeches in front of people you've never met who decide if you're worth it, if you're good enough.

Most Drama Schools take on about 30 people every year and have between 1,000 and 3,000 people applying for these 30 places. This immediately means that the vast, overwhelming majority of applicants have to fail. I would learn some speeches (including one by Roderigo in Othello, an excellent play – ask your English teacher about it!) and then travel into London to audition for a place. As you can imagine, each audition was nerve-wracking as I really wanted to impress the people on the panel (imagine something like Britain's Got Talent but with no audience and, mercifully, no buzzers) so that I could come back and audition again in front of more important people who could possibly let me in to their Drama School to train as an actor.

I failed. I failed lots of times. I did some speeches I thought were quite good, I did some other speeches that I thought were really good, I tried and I tried and I tried and then a few weeks later I'd get a letter in the post saying 'We're very sorry but…' I failed. I failed a lot. I kept going for three years. Three years is a long time! I kept going, I kept trying, and I didn't give up even though it was really tiring and, to be honest, upsetting to have people I didn't know writing to tell me I wasn't good enough. I can promise that each and every failure was worth it because when I finally got accepted (a) it taught me that even if people say I can't do something, I can prove that I can and (b) the skills and experience I developed at Drama School changed me in lots of ways that still help me now (you may have noticed I have quite a loud, powerful voice… I was taught how to use it).

Skipping forward a few years, I'd decided to become a Maths Teacher and applied to lots of different schools in Reading, Henley and, of course, Didcot… I used to work as a private maths tutor before I became a Maths Teacher and so when I first came to Didcot Girls' School back in 2013 to have an interview, I'd never taught maths in a classroom before. It showed. My lesson, if I'm honest, was really rather rubbish and I failed to get a job as a Maths Teacher at Didcot Girls' School. I was absolutely gutted because not only had I worked really, really hard on that lesson (I'd spent all weekend on it) but I'd known really quickly that DGS was a school I wanted to work in, so you can imagine how disappointed and upset I was when I got the phone call telling me I hadn't got the job.

I didn't let this failure put me off, however. I learned a lot from the experience and the feedback about the lesson, became better at maths teaching and got a job in a different school. It was a good school but I wanted to work here… Two years later, in 2015, I summoned up the courage to apply to this wonderful school which had rejected me, this school that I'd failed in applying to, this school that suddenly had a Maths Teacher job going… and I got the job, beating three other teachers, all of whom were really good (it was not an easy day).

Both of these failures have taught me a lot about myself as a person. They've taught me that persevering when I got something wrong was really important and, crucially, listening to people who knew more than I did would help me get better and stand a greater chance of success. It can be quite difficult to admit that you've got something wrong and ask for help to get better – I promise that if you go through life with a good, positive attitude and you have the humility to ask for help from people who know what they're talking about and if you don't let individual failures in your life stop you, then you will surprise yourself with what you can achieve. Whether it's disappointment in a test result, not getting into a sports team, or school production or just not achieving something you want the very first time you try it – if you don't let failure stop you, then you have no idea what you can achieve in your life.

I wish you all the luck in the world in bouncing back from your failures and I'd love to hear how you've overcome these and moved forwards.

Miss Landsbert, School Psychologist

My friend and I were having lunch one day a few months back, when she said she was going to attempt the National Three Peaks Challenge. This was something I had always wanted to do, especially as I'd been poorly the year, I had the opportunity to do my Bronze D of E at school. The National Three Peaks Challenge involves climbing the highest peaks of each country in the UK within a 24-hour window (including travelling between then). That's 23 miles of walking all up or down hill, and the equivalent of over 1,000 flights of stairs. Ben Nevis in Scotland, Scafell Pike in England, and Snowdon in Wales. You have to do at least one mountain in the dark in order to achieve this feat, and it's best to have a mountain guide with you and someone else doing the driving! In short, it's a huge undertaking.

Before I knew it, my friend had asked her colleagues if I, a complete stranger to the rest of them, could join them on their epic adventure. When they said yes, I could barely contain my excitement and the necessary three months of training up and down hills was underway, as was research into how much to eat, how bright the head torch needs to be, etc.

So when half term came, I was watching the weather forecast like I've never watched it before. South of England 23 degrees sunny – lovely weekend, people in paddling pools and on beaches. As we set off, everyone was saying "enjoy the views". Scotland, Wales, and the North of England?!? Rain, cold, and high winds! So, I packed a complete change of clothes (five layers) for each mountain.

We had planned to start walking at midday, after a good night's sleep. However, the weather meant that the best (and safest) window for climbing Ben Nevis was to be off the mountain by breakfast time... so we started climbing the mountain at 3 a.m. Three hours later (that's quick by the way), it was cold at the top. There's no group photo, and no views. Perhaps disappointing? Just me on my own. The advance party had already headed down the mountain because it was too cold. With everyone needing a dry set of clothes and a hot drink, we were late leaving, and our goal of 24 hours was already behind us. Had we failed?

Driving to Scafell Pike was initially going well, when we were all woken by a BANG – a coach had knocked the wing mirror off the minibus and showered half the party in glass. We stopped for three and a half hours to sort this out and got to Scafell Pike later than planned. It was still raining, but a human chain got us across the swollen river. Then, I fell up hill and landed with my whole-body weight on my right knee. OUCH! I was up a mountain, wet through, and it was so dark and misty you can't see anyone else's torches. We were stopping every few minutes to regroup and head count. Thank goodness for our Qualified Mountain Guide. We found other people up the mountain without one, and they shared our guide down.

There are no photos of me on this mountain. Does this mean I won't remember it? There was however hot food on a camping stove at the bottom of the mountain – That was the best midnight feast ever!

Having had only seven hours sleep in three nights, been wet through five layers twice, and with a very bruised knee, I decided not to climb the third mountain. We'd been very unlucky with the weather and effectively I had failed to me meet my goal.

However, for me, there is no way that I have failed. In the process of trying and not quite reaching my goal, I have achieved rather a lot:

- While training, I realised that I am far more content with my own company than I thought I was. If I hadn't learned that I can go and do exercise on my own, I would never have experienced a baby badger pootling across the path in front of me... not 3 metres away – that was a heart stoppingly awesome experience in itself

- I've never been fitter in my life

- I've aspired to be up a mountain at dawn for a while – There was no sunrise up Ben Nevis, but I was in awe to see the shapes of the mountains emerging from the mist and darkness

- On Ben Nevis, I was the highest person in the UK for a whole five minutes – that wouldn't have happened if the others hadn't already left because it was so cold

- On Scafell Pike, I overcame the fear of wading through a mountain river – that wouldn't have happened if it hadn't been raining... and somehow it seemed easier on the way back too, even though it was dark and my knee was REALLY hurting

- I climbed the two highest and hardest mountains and they only took about five hours each in the most appalling weather I've ever experienced and with a dodgy knee. Not many people do that – it's usually a bit easier!

- I've raised a really pleasing amount of money for a charity which supports people through their teenage years and into adulthood

There aren't many pictures of my trip – it was basically either raining or dark... but there are still lots of memories which will never leave me.

Have I failed? No ... but I am looking for a friend who'd like to climb Snowdon with me... preferably in the daylight and hopefully with some views.

So, I think what I'm trying to convey is plan and work hard to meet your goals and take the right people with you on your journey. But if you don't quite reach your goal, think about what you have achieved and learned in the process, and be proud. I am.

PS My knee is getting better every day.

Where grit and leadership work in tandem, and we pursue our dreams head on, failure is inevitable. As educators, we must find ways to teach our students not to worry too much about failure, reminding them with sincerity that where there is success, failure is very likely to be experienced too. Like anything we find uncomfortable, it won't go away if we fear it, nor if we stay in a state of denial about it. So why wish it away and why let it bully us? Failure, from time to time, is inevitable. There is much to be gained from accepting this reality in our pursuit of success.

Tool kit

- Talk about failure and risk-taking openly and wholesomely to the school community

- Normalise vulnerability to allow young people to feel validated

- Tell your own stories of failure and growth to reassure and to inspire young people

- Find creative ways to encourage reflection and self-growth

- When modelling responses, allow students access to your mistakes and corrections

7 Outward facing schools

Read on to: find out why outward facing schools are so successful at raising globally aware conscious leaders who understand the world around them and their role within it. Explore the ways in which schools can embark on the journey to becoming more outward facing.

Bringing the outside in

If there is one thing my role at the Trust has taught me, it is that by bringing the outside world into the classroom, schools offer young people the best life chances in the future. Schools can be outward facing in several ways: strong links to parents, the local community, the wider community, the national and international community – these connections allow our young people to feel empowered and supported, while in a safe and familiar setting. Connecting students to the wider world, mobilising them and hence enhancing their future chances is even more important where families are not able to provide such links as easily. Research is clear that outward facing schools are much more likely to nurture individuals who make a positive contribution to society in the future. Over the following pages, I suggest ways in which schools can become more outward facing in their approach, while acknowledging that different schools will need to prioritise this aspect of ethos in accordance with their needs. School leaders must become more creative about bringing the community, the country, and the world into their schools in meaningful and inclusive ways. The range of possibilities may include adding a global dimension to lessons and assemblies, overseas visits for staff and students (virtually conducted if necessary), global fellowships, school pairings, festivals, cooperatives, charities, youth worker schemes, family workshops, newsletters, community radio, holiday activities, sponsorships, and university visits. Many schools are already well on their way to becoming outward facing, some

DOI: 10.4324/9781003275985-7

are already there (thought I would argue there is no 'end-point' on this journey) and no doubt some have not begun this journey. My hope it that this chapter is valuable no matter where you are on the journey to become a truly outward facing school.

What does it mean to be an outward facing school?

Being an outward facing school is essentially about looking out beyond the school community and into the broader world, ranging from the local community, the county, the country, and ultimately the world. An outward facing school recognises that in order to nurture well-rounded and socially aware individuals, an awareness of the world around them is an essential starting point. Depending on where it is situated, the school community can feel quite small and removed from the outside world. While there is clearly nothing to be done about this geographically speaking, there is so much schools can do to bring the 'outside in' throughout the year. When a school is outward facing, its community has a clear and compassionate understanding of the world, the different cultures it comprises, a sense of geopolitical developments and an understanding of 'sameness in difference'. Keeping this ethos at the fore of our minds can pave the way to achieving equality, diversity, and inclusion in the truest sense of the word. Beyond this, a meaningful understanding of the world allows young people to consider their own position within it and encourages them to contemplate the contribution they may make to it. A deeper knowledge of different cultures is ultimately essential if young people are to feel comfortable with what may seem different or unfamiliar – I am hard pressed to think of a more important lesson than this to teach our children in these times. Young people's interactions with a range of social groups are intrinsically linked to their attitude to difference, and schools have the privilege of playing a significant role here: to make their world's constantly bigger and their understanding of it infinitely deeper. We then begin to make critical thinking and analysis more accessible to our students – skills that they will take into the world and use to navigate their lives both professionally and personally.

Even a decade ago, Deputy Head Teacher Jose Picardo wrote in *The Guardian*:

Global awareness and international collaboration during the formative years results in more rounded individuals, encouraging our pupils to see things from different perspectives and helping them to make informed decisions, acquiring transferable skills that will be useful to them and will remain with them for life. According to the Association of Graduate Recruiters companies cannot find enough applicants with the requisite skills to operate in an international marketplace, indicating that greater efforts by schools in fostering global awareness and international collaboration are needed to best prepare our students – and ourselves – for life in the 21st century.

(Picardo, 2012)

International links

According to survey conducted by *Tes* and the British Council "UK teachers were concerned about the lack of international opportunities in their schools". Of the over 2,220 staff who were consulted, "just 37 per cent felt that their pupils had a good understanding of cultures other than their own, while more than half said that pupils' interest in modern foreign languages was declining in their school" (Shaw, n.d.). I know that many others, like me, will find this to be less than ideal. Sadly, school trips are not the solution that many are hoping for. School trips abroad are undoubtedly exciting and memorable, but not always feasible in the consistent way. In my 14 years at school, I went to one school trip abroad and I distinctly remember that I was one of just 30 students who managed to go. School trips are not consistent and are not the answer for everyone. However, there are other ways which allow us to benefit from those exciting links with international schools without ever actually visiting them. These alliances can make a real difference to our students. They can help:

- To encourage students to understand the lives and cultures of other young people
- To broaden their horizons and widen their perspectives
- To learn to appreciate difference and seek common ground
- To create networks and forge friendships
- To develop a global consciousness, culturally, geographically, and politically
- To pique their curiosities and interests

Languages

Sandra Cohen, our Head of German, recently won us the International Schools Award. I knew it would be worth talking to her to gain her insights and expertise for the purpose of this chapter. As a bonus, I also ended up having one of the most fascinating conversations I have had with a colleague in a while. Sandra was born and grew up in Holland, speaking fluent Dutch (of course!) and with English as a second language. As part of her 16 + secondary school education, Sandra chose to study Dutch, Spanish, French, and German – alongside her other subjects! Considering most people pick no more than four A Level subjects in the UK, this fact alone left me completely in awe. Sandra believes that both as a language teacher and a member of the school community, it is her responsibility to open students' eyes what is happening in the world around them. This knowledge, she believes, is the right of every student. While the department of modern foreign languages teach German, French, Spanish, and Mandarin, the learning they impart reaches far beyond the acquisition of language; Sandra takes great pride in the fact that her students learn about the geography, topography, culture, and people who speak these languages as their mother tongue. Students in her German class have a Christmas biscuit making tradition, as part of which they must research the different sorts of biscuits made by German families and settle on a recipe they feel partial to. These contributions are brought into school first after judge and for everyone to enjoy. They learn about the origin off the Austrian Sacher torte in Year 10 as part of their topic "I love Vienna". Maps are a central feature of Sandra's classroom because she is passionate about using her subject to bring the world to the young people of Didcot. On a wider scale level, Sandra and her team organise an annual International Day which is an outreach opportunity to two local primary schools who were invited to visit a school in our Trust. This daylong event not only allows children to forge a link with their future school but is a wonderful daylong opportunity to experience flavour of up to seven different cultures. They are provided a passport upon arrival and have these stamped as they visit different arenas, all of which represent a different country. The day features everything from learning traditional German dancing to making Chinese fans and trying out Japanese kimonos to sampling French food. In addition to all of this, International Day offers a range of excellent leadership opportunities to our Year 8 students who are tour guides for the day.

Other major international aspects of the Modern Foreign Languages Department include the annual German exchange visit arranged between us and our German partner school. The experience of attending a German school for a week, living with a German family and having so much exposure to the culture and language is an unforgettable experience for our students. Some of these students have never flown on a plane and may not do again for a while yet; we have had students report that this trip has been one of the greatest highlights of their lives so far. Sandra did add the disclaimer that unless time and effort is invested in networking and relationship building, these exchange visits can be challenging to arrange for staff, which is worth bearing in mind in advance.

In addition, Year 9 experience the Digital Exchange programme which uses Microsoft Teams as the platform for communication. This runs over five weeks and invites students (who are partnered based on similar interests and hobbies) to connect weekly using a predetermined theme. This can be anything from a discussion about favourite cities to music to food and films. I was intrigued to know that students are encouraged to communicate in their language of choice;

this flexibility allows the freedom to be themselves and enables a strong connection to develop.

Languages, then, are a fantastic way to grow our outward facing stance at schools and I left Sandra's classroom with no doubt that the curiosity and spark created by the study of languages is an invaluable gift. There is nothing more satisfying to me than the moments from ethos and learning merge, and this is a beautiful example of just that.

Media Studies, for example

Using the example of Media Studies in particular might appear to be a very niche choice. However, it does happen to be a subject that I am particularly passionate about and even if you don't offer this as an option at your school, there are several other significant ways in which media can be weaved into the fabric of our school systems. Some experts argue that Media Studies might just be the most important subject we can teach and learn now. Having plenty of personal experience of teaching Media Studies to Year 9 and 10, I can say with conviction that done right, the subject goes a long way to contribute to an outward facing mindset. In addition to providing opportunities to explore global developments, Media Studies allows students to understand reality's many 'versions' and examine the ways in which mass communication represents individuals, cultures, and communities. Developing critical thinking skills at an early age, particularly when it comes to digital media (which the average teenager engages with for eight hours a day) supports our understanding of how we view and access the world. If your school happens to teach Media Studies already, perhaps the link between the subject and its direct correlation with global consciousness among young people is worth reiterating. I have frequently dealt with questions regarding the validity of Media Studies and why it is at all different to accessing the media in our private lives. The answer lies plainly in analysis. No matter how we decide to go about this at schools, it is important that we find windows of opportunity where we can educate young people about how the media controls, dictates, and often manipulates their understanding of the world and its people. I like addressing near stories as quickly and responsively as I can through 'ethos bites' in tutor time, a focus group in the library or indeed a staple for many schools – assemblies. Yes, we want our schools and students to be outward facing, but they need to be simultaneously armed with the confidence to question what they see in here and the curiosity that makes them one to probe.

Outreach work

A few years ago, our wonderfully proactive school council expressed an interest in working with an international charity. Our research led us to a UK-based charity called The African Children's Fund; their mission is summarised on their website as follows:

African Children's Fund was founded in 2006 by Dee and Peter Tyrer to sup-
port local initiatives to benefit under-served children. The projects we support
are run by local staff who are committed to – and know the needs of – their own
communities.

Africa's children need an education if Africa is to prosper. That is why we focus
on giving children what they need to get that education which in turn gives them
hope for a bright future.

It was the Head Teacher at a school in Kenya who told us what stops children
attending his school: the first is a lack of food in the family, meaning children have
to work, scavenge or beg on the streets during the day, or be hungry at school. The
second is the un-affordability of sanitary protection for girls, forcing them to miss
a week of school each month (African Children's Fund, n.d.).

As a girls' school, we responded to this initiative straight away. Before any official fundraising began, we had the opportunity to find out a little more than we knew about countries such as Zambia, Kenya, Tanzania, and Uganda. We began to try to know a culture we had very little idea about and it felt like a steep and very rewarding learning curve. The links that formed, stemming initially from the idea of our school helping a school in Tanzania, helped us more than we could ever imagine. As schools, we always talk about readying our students for the world; perhaps we need to 'show' them the world better as a first step.

Another recent instance of linking up with the country that feels very far away and different to ours was our decision to support flood victims in rural Pakistan. We raised funds over the course of a few weeks but alongside made a concerted effort to understand Pakistan, its different regions, its many languages, its location and how this impacts the country as well as its geopolitical positioning in the world. We have several students who are British Pakistani and felt empowered that we were talking about this country with a view to genuinely finding out more about it; for others, it felt like a steep but important learning curve.

The football World Cup in Qatar is approaching its knockout stages as I write this chapter. Young people at our Trust are very enthused about it and even the ones who have little interest are aware of the key moments around it. They regularly ask us to play the matches during lessons – which we politely refuse to do – and lunch and break times are abuzz with conversations about the matches on the day. Despite all the fervour, there seems to be an ignorance about the host nation, Qatar, including a reluctance to learn how to pronounce it accurately. This does not come from a place of malice but from ignorance and lack of familiarity. To me, this presents an opportunity to enlighten our young people and encourage them to feel more comfortable in the world around them.

Tim Smith makes a great case for becoming more 'outward facing' as schools
when he describes schools as a 'massive safety net'. He writes on:

*If you're not connecting things, then there are going to be holes and kids are go-
ing to fall through. Bringing the outside world into the classroom and connecting
the school to the wider community in every way possible is just as important as formal learning. If we imagine that these connections form nets then the more there
are, the smaller the gaps there will be and the harder it will be for anyone to slip
through. They believed that education should connect young people to the wider
world. They recognised that the school's role was particularly important where
families may not be well placed to establish such links. Many of the Fellows' passion was driven by an appreciation of how deprived their students were. One said,
Our knowledge of the home circumstances of many of our students makes it clear
to us that we have to mobilise and engage parents, carers and the local community
as fully as we can, in our efforts to raise their achievement and improve their life
chances* (Bubb, n.d.).

Careers

Careers and personal development has grown to become one of the most credible
strengths at the Trust in the past decade or so. Didcot Girls' School is one of two
schools in Oxfordshire to have achieved all seven of the Gatsby Benchmarks.

Our school has a network of department-based 'Careers Champions' who lead
on Careers in the Curriculum initiatives. The group aims to meet three times each
year with a view to:

- Raise pupils' careers aspirations

- Broaden pupils' knowledge of careers that exist linked to their curriculum
  learning

- Increase motivation for pupils to succeed in their subjects

- Ensure pupils are informed regarding GCSE's, Further and Higher Education
  options and Careers Examples of actions to-date include:

  - Department-based careers conferences and careers fairs

  - Career displays in departments

  - Subject-based career 'wordles'

  - Department careers posters

  - Showcasing job profiles linked to department subjects

  - Employee visits and online talks

The following information is shared with the local community and beyond, to
share our work on careers and invite further involvement. The outward facing

nature of this provision has meant that our students benefit from a powerful combination of in-house training and external expertise:

One specific partnership we value with many local employers is the provision of work experience. Currently, our students benefit from a two-week work experience programme in the summer term of Year 10 each year. If you would like to contact us regarding work experience, then our Work Experience Co-ordinator would be delighted to hear from you. Other specific areas we are interested in developing with local businesses are: Takeover Challenge Days, which are effectively one-day work experience placements for Year 7s and Year 9s. These are always good fun for all involved and a great opportunity for students to learn hands on about the world of work and for companies to engage with young people and promote their own sector or even gain a young person's perspective on their company and/or products or services. Mentoring for our Sixth Form – If you are able to offer your time, knowledge, and expertise to mentor one of our Sixth Form students, for three sessions, then we would welcome your participation in one of our most impactful careers initiatives we run. Sixth Form Work Experience – Are you able to support our Sixth Form students with their university or employment applications, by offering work experience or work placement opportunities, that will enable them to apply and/ or practise in a practical context their theoretical learning. Speaker – Would you be available to offer your support as a speaker on an ad hoc basis? This could be to deliver a talk, run a short workshop, or even provide a tour at your own business. Participation at our Year 11 and Year 12 Careers Conventions is also a possibility if you would like to promote a Career/Sector or pathway.

I have captured the context of Careers provision in an interview I conducted with my colleague, Stuart George, who leads on Careers and Personal Development at the Trust.

ME: Stuart, what inspired you to become the Head of Careers?

STUART: I arrived in the role without really aiming to get it; I was young and ambitious, and the school was looking for a Careers' lead. This was ten years ago, around 2012. Our Careers provision was minimal, and we needed to build from scratch. It felt like an opportunity, and I was keen to take on more responsibility. That's how the journey began.

ME: How do you make Careers exciting for young people, even when they are possibly too young to be thinking very seriously about their careers?

STUART: I am invested in building links between employers and young people and am constantly building up a network of employers who we can turn to, either to come in and deliver a talk or workshop, or to send our students to them for work experience and Take Over Days. This makes Careers more 'real' and exciting for students. Also, I design 'off timetable days' to be varied and memorable, so that our students look forward to being involved in these. These can be little things – I have recoded a video of the Senior Leadership Team talking about their careers, set up pupil voice survey to be send out during the day so that students can instantly respond using their phones, making the process highly interactive, and am careful to build an element of fun into all activities I plan.

ME: How do you ensure that the Careers provision you offer is not just high quality but exceptional?

STUART: The work I do takes huge amounts of organisation, planning, and networking. When this is done meticulously at my end, I can keep the messages for staff and students simple. Simplicity is key given how much else everyone is juggling. I tell people only what they need to know, which means the focus is never lost and the messages are retained. We send out hundreds of students for Take Over Days off-site, even as early as Year 7. Most of our students avail this offer, which I facilitate by being the link between the school and the employer, though, of course, students are asked to find a place of work themselves. Those who are unable to procure a place then come to me, where using my data base I can connect them with an employer. This can feel like a daunting ambition – the idea of having up to 300 students out for Take Over Day – so simplicity and clarity of communication must be key. Over the years, I have also become very conscious of attaining feedback from students about experience of Careers straight after an event or session. This enables me to improve our offer on an ongoing basis.

ME: How do you keep staff on board with the Careers provision?

STUART: I do this mainly by keeping the positives of a strong Careers education in the narrative at all times: sharing highlights and photos of recent events, so that staff can see their students (even those who are less amenable to classroom leaning) thrive in other settings, distil key facts about upcoming calendared events in a timely way, talk to them regularly about the moral purpose of this work, and yes essentially, keep sharing the 'good stuff'.

ME: And what happens once our students join the Sixth Form?

STUART: Our Careers' offer continues well into Sixth Form. We have a systemised approach which covers everything from Careers Research, University Research, and Student Finance to Apprenticeship and Employment after Sixth Form, voluntary work, gap years, and more generalised careers advice.

Thinking creatively and carefully about ways to make our young people's worlds bigger is an incredibly rewarding process and has proved to be one of the most enjoyable aspects of my job. The links we can develop will reap rewards for years to come and the curiosity we plant in young minds will only ever get deeper as they progress on their leadership journeys.

Tool kit

- Arrive at a clear sense of ways in which your school can become more outward facing

- Share the reasons for why being outward facing is important with staff, students, and parents

- Make outreach work with charities abroad a priority

- Consider links with international schools and organisations to broaden an understanding of the wider world

- Use subjects such as Modern Foreign Languages and Media Studies to enhance students' global awareness

- Ensure that your career's provision is robust and exciting, as well as consistent in its pledge to enhance life opportunities for young people

8 The ethos calendar

Read on: to discover how a strategic and well-thought-out enrichment plan works to promote ethos and leadership in an inclusive way. This chapter offers suggestions on how to plan an eclectic range of events, privileging school values and priorities, in an enjoyable and powerful way.

It can be tempting to assume that a positive exciting and diverse school culture is the happy by-product of existing systems at school. A robust and visionary senior leadership team, excellent provisions for teaching, learning and pastoral care are undoubtedly the pillars needed to support a positive culture. However, in order to deliver a broad-based and diverse wider school experience, a good deal of thinking and planning needs to be done well before the start of the year. I called this system the ethos calendar. The following pages explore how the ethos calendar is designed, the different variables considered when creating it, how the context of the school, that country and the world are taken into consideration when planning, and a vision for how staff and students come together to realise this vision. The ethos calendar typically incorporates a whole host of items: these can range from student leadership training days, workshops delivered by external experts, charity events, house competitions, global awareness days and weeks, religious festivals, student conferences, and guest speaker visits. Here, I go into details about all these aspects of the ethos calendar as well as the rationale behind them and the impact they create.

There are two aspects of the ethos calendar that are worth mentioning at the outset: one, our use of the 'Thought for the term' in structuring events within the calendar, and second, the importance of putting inclusion at the heart of our planning. The thought for the term, detailed below, is incredibly useful in enabling school leaders to design and frame events, activities, and assemblies within a term and avoid our messages become mixed and too confusing. It serves as a powerful

 DOI: 10.4324/9781003275985-8

thread that runs through the term and keeps us all aligned in our values. Now to my second point: in the world of education, at least in the UK, it has become fashionable to talk about 'tilting our systems' to become inclusive. I think we can go a step beyond this. I think we need to speak the language of building our systems and not tilting our systems to cater to our most disadvantage students. If we want enrichment and young leadership to be meaningful and inclusive as opposed to elitist and exclusive, inclusion must be front and centre in our thinking. One of the reasons why the Trust enjoys such an inclusive, exciting, and varied ethos is that we create a powerful and dynamic 'ethos calendar'. We do the thinking beforehand rather than reactively. Each year, I am in awe of the incredible impact this pre-planning has on our student body.

For clarity, I have divided this chapter into five major segments:

● How thought for the term works and what it encompasses

● How to mark and celebrate global awareness days through the school year

● How to plan and structure assemblies effectively through the school year

● Highlights of the ethos calendar

● A note on planning successful schoolwide events

Thought for the term

Having a thought or value to frame each term enables us to focus on a wide and eclectic range of values, without becoming exclusively tethered to the main school values which are our staples through the year. Having been in place now for over a decade, the thought for the term allows us to be responsive and creative to how the world is unfolding around us too. We start of the school year in September with a focus on **vision** and setting goals; we invite students to set tangible goals for success as well more intangible and personal ones, such as remembering to practice gratitude and investing in their well-being. In January, in keeping with our cold weather and the end of the festive season, we tend to explore **self-care and well-being**, inviting students to consider the different ways we can infuse our lives with joy and fun, just for the sake of joy and fun! Before public examinations, we often address feelings of **vulnerability** and the **fear of failure**: our aim is to normalise these feelings and accept that we all, from time to time, experience vulnerability. My students have always experienced an 'aha!' moment when I have introduced them to the notion of vulnerability being, not only inevitable sometimes, but also empowering. Brene Brown's rich and powerful study on vulnerability helps me communicate this concept with clarity and passion. In *Daring Greatly*, Brown describes vulnerability as "uncertainty, risk, and emotional exposure" and goes on to explain that "Vulnerability is not winning or losing; it's having the courage to show up and be seen when we have no control over the outcome. Vulnerability is not weakness; it's our greatest measure of courage" (Brown, 2012).

The Thought for the Term framework allows us to pass these important life messages on to young people in a natural, wholesome, and effective way. Each week of the term, a member of staff or student leader writes an inspirational entry based on the 'thought'. These are shared widely within the school community and beyond. They are deliberately written to be accessible and enjoyable to all secondary school age groups – and importantly, their families. I receive regular communication from parents to say how much they enjoyed reading a Thought for the Term and how it offered a real opportunity for dinner table discussions with their young people. What more can we ask for?

As mentioned previously, one summer, we decided to choose 'Failure' as our thought for the term. There had been whisperings about student anxiety around mock exams, and we gained a general sense the words *failing* and *failure* itself were being used rather liberally and not in an open and enabling way. There seemed little point in shying away from the idea of failure; it was clearly playing on our students' minds and so we decided to embrace it fully and unabashedly. Each week, a senior member of staff would write an inspiring message, allowing students to consider failure in all its nuances and complexity. To give this a more personal dimension, and to really form a connection with our students, I tentatively suggested to staff if some of them would consider sharing a personal story of failure, and how they dealt with it, or perhaps changed as a result of it. This resulted in a booklet which we entitled *The Chronicles of Failure*: a resource still talked about today many years later, and one which students found incredibly powerful and refreshing. I share a selection of these in the previous chapter.

My experience strongly suggests that when it comes to picking a thought or value to frame a term, it is important to be agile and responsive, selecting what works well for you as a school as well as keeping ethos fresh and exciting. Alongside this, it is worth collating student voice regularly to establish a sense of how much impact these initiatives are having on them. At the Trust, we make students part of this process and include them in our rota of contributors; for us, it has meant that the weekly entries are widely read and circulated too. I have included an extensive selection of our thoughts for the term later in the book (they are joyous and uplifting to read!), but here are a couple of examples straight away:

Thought for the term: creativity

There is a prevalent myth that some people are creative, and others aren't and, in the context of education, that some subjects are creative and others aren't. I don't agree. I believe creativity is synonymous with inventiveness. It is making something new from the pieces of your knowledge. It requires flexibility and responsiveness. It requires thinking hard on topics so that you create your own viewpoint or opinion. It is not without discipline. In fact, subjects such as music, dance, cooking, writing, design technology, and drama all need high levels of skill and lots of practice. Doing scales or bar exercises everyday might not seem very creative. Sitting alone at a laptop for hours might not seem very creative. But that time and those skills are important foundations for the creations which are to follow. To take an example, I have written a novel. It is about 80,000 words long. Some experiences of writing it fit in with a stereotypical idea of 'creativity'. I had one (just one) day in the 18 months or so of working on it when I wrote 4,500 words in an unbelievable rush. It is true that many times when I sat down to it, I did experience a strange power of momentum as the next sentence emerged and the next and then the next, which at times did feel mysterious and I was literally creating sentences and paragraphs and chapters out of thin air. But I've been reading books for 40 years and I have an English literature degree. And I needed the discipline and deadlines and feedback of my teacher and writing group to actually make me write it. And I took time away from work to free up enough space in my head for the hard thinking required. And I spend a lot of hours crafting and redrafting. My mysterious creativity didn't come from nowhere. Opportunities for creativity are everywhere in school. Are you using the knowledge you have been taught in Maths and Science to solve problems which you have never previously encountered? Are you asking questions and seeking to expand your knowledge in Geography to apply it to the new situations which you see developing in the world around us? Are you taking an active role in your own learning, experimenting and taking risks so that you can achieve more in Art? Are you building your vocabulary in English and then using new words to make your writing more engaging? Are you practising your skills in Music and Drama and Dance to take your performances to new heights? If the answer is yes to any of these, then you are harnessing your powers of creativity too!

Mrs Bowers
Deputy Headteacher St Birinus School

Thought for the term: fresh starts

The beginning of a new academic year brings about a plethora of changes. From changing year group to school to teachers. With each change, there is a new set of pressures and expectations. We tend to fear this change. There is an evolutionary basis for this – humans are wired to value routine and consistency because it ensured resources and the best chance of survival. So, thousands of years ago, we deduced that remaining in the same position meant safety and security. If that's the case if it's our instinctual response to veer away from change, why have we changed? Why do we change? It comes down to one word – opportunity. While every change brings risk, it also poses an opportunity. Perhaps it's that humanity will transition to a new metal that will completely change how the world functions or a new idea that will transform medicine. Or perhaps, it will be a new method learnt, a new friend made, a new role available. Whether big or small, every change brings the opportunity for a fresh start and growth, personal or collective.

This is not to diminish our fear of change. Arguably, it is this human tendency to remain consistent and honour our past that has led to our traditions that have been passed down from generation to generation. This was clearly displayed recently following the passing of Queen Elizabeth II and the communal respect and appreciation for her life and work, despite the world changing drastically in the last 70 years. Furthermore, is it not the risk we take and the fear we feel when making a change that makes the ultimate reward all the more satisfying?

Queen Elizabeth II once said,

Whatever life throws at us, our individual response will be all the stronger for working together to share the load. We can learn from this. As a school community, let us embrace the change of a new academic year and the opportunities it brings. Together, let us embrace a fresh start.

Nina O'Hanlon, Kennedy House Captain

Marking global awareness days/weeks/month

People are often unsure about having a day, a week, or a month to mark something important. Admittedly, this concept has been taken to somewhat silly levels recently – national umbrella day, toss a fruit cake day, bubble bath day, dress your pet up day, and squirrel appreciation day all exist now. While some of these do pique my curiosity, I can't deny but when picking awareness days on our ethos calendar, discretion reigns supreme! Once again, school values are a good place to start when determining which days we wish to mark as a school community. As a school, respect, high expectations, and inclusion are all incredibly important to us so we are always cognizant of finding ways to mark and promote any awareness days but align with these values. Examples include International Women's Day, International Men's Day, International Day of the Girl Child, Anti-Bullying Week, Remembrance Day, Holocaust Memorial Day, Earth Day, LGBTQ+ History Month, Prode Month, Black History Month, Disability History Awareness Month, Mental Health Awareness Week, International Animal Rights Awareness Day – there are more, but this is a selection of the most important ones. How we chose to mark these awareness days can be varied and will depend on how dense the school calendar feels at the time. There are times when it makes more sense to have just lower school involved in an event; there are times when the most straightforward approach is to send out an activity to tutor time; there are times when we wish to get the entire school involved at scale and there are yet other times when we want to promote an idea purely visually, through screens around school, artwork, posters, and display boards. Having a range of options is always a good idea as not only does it create more flexibility, but it also keeps the school ethos energetic and interesting. As you read on, you will see that I go into more detail about some of these events, including the more challenging organisational aspects.

Assemblies

Assemblies can be one of our most powerful tools as educators, so it's important to use them wisely, creatively, and regularly. A dull assembly, or one that is delivered half-heartedly, is a real shame and a regrettable waste of 20 minutes' worth of audience with young people – 20 minutes is a luxury; if you ask me, even 5 minutes is powerful. It's a privilege which I have grown to value deeply. In my role, I ensure that any assemblies planned by me or my team are of an exceptional standard. If we want our students to spend 20 minutes first thing in the morning listening to us in a hall (often in the cold, sometimes seated on the floor), the least we can do is make it worthwhile. During lock down and in its aftermath, I have found that virtual assemblies have an important role to play so as a Trust we have not shied away from turning to these frequently even after they have stopped being mandated. The time saved in lining up and registering students is precious indeed, especially when you have a complex or profound topic to cover. I am by no means in favour of dispensing with in-person assemblies, but it does not have to be a case of 'either-or'. Students need a space to understand what is unfolding around them in a safe space from people they trust. They don't need to be swayed or influenced but rather just armed with knowledge – knowledge is power, and this is important to convey to them. Experience has taught me that when handling difficult subjects, it is important to do our research carefully and consult colleagues; have senior leaders support you, so you are not isolated in case there is any parental backlash. Later on in the book, I include templates of assemblies I have delivered, some of which may feel dated by the time you are reading this, but will nonetheless offer a glimpse into planning, organisation, and tips for engagement.

When it comes to deciding the structure of assemblies within a school year, a careful balancing act is important to strike. There will be assemblies that staff and senior leaders will deliver as a matter of course during the school year, year on year. These assemblies will include everything from behaviour, learning habits, health and safety, road safety, choosing subject options, exploring school values – It is a fairly comprehensive list. However, there are times in the year when as school leaders we must respond to a significant situation that may arise. I see it very much as our responsibility to help young people make sense of challenging, sensitive, or unexpected local and global events that often occur with little notice. My colleagues and I have often been in a position where we have had to plan, quality assure, and deliver an assembly with less than 24 hours' notice. Examples from recent years include an assembly I had to prepare during lockdown to capture the events unfolding in the Israel versus Palestine crisis in the

Middle East. As schools, we are expected to remain politically and ideologically neutral – planning an assembly to convey the gravity and the sensitivities of this crisis, along with the complex history behind it, in a span of 15 minutes felt like a daunting challenge. How could I maintain neutrality when my views on the situation were all too clear to me? Was I knowledgeable enough on this complex topic? Would I be offending anyone's sensitivities through what I said? Just these thoughts and trepidations were enough to make me consider whether the assembly was a good idea at all. Ultimately, I decided that if as schools we are not brave enough to explore difficult subject matters with our young people, then we are leaving it to a host of other sources to play this part; yes, I am confident that the vast majority of parents are able to have these conversations patiently and sensitively with their children, but experience also shows us that we can never take this for granted. Our students are heavily reliant on social media as a news source, and we need to ensure that a clear and balanced picture, grounded in accuracy, is made available to them through us. Other such occasions for responsive assemblies have arisen in recent times: Russia's attack on Ukraine and its ongoing impact on the world's population, the ideological controversies that surrounded the football World Cup in Qatar, the protests over the role of the morality police in Iran, and the banning of school for girls in Afghanistan in 2021. As schools, we have a responsibility to help our students make sense of such developments and sometimes the best thing to do is to have our school community in the hall, united by common values, learning about the world and its people. While in general my advice is to have a full set of assemblies populated in school calendar before the start of the year and ensure that staff and students know to expect these, we also need to be prepared to be flexible and responsive – to expect and welcome an opportunity to help our student body reflect on something powerful that may have unfolded.

Highlights of the ethos calendar

Student leadership conference: International Men's Day and International Women's Day

Our annual student leadership conference has become a much looked forward to tradition at the Trust. We hold two every year: one to mark International Women's Day (8th March) and another to mark International Men's Day (19th November). Both days have a predetermined theme which allows us to frame our event and guide our guest speakers. In the past, we have had themes such as:

#pressforprogress (2018)

#balanceforbetter (2019)

#eachforequal (2020)

#choosetochallenge (2021)

#breakthebias (2022)

International Men's Day is a more recent development and organisers have established themes linked to wholesome masculinity, mental health, equality, and a range of approaches that can make a difference to the lives of men and boys.

The conference does take careful planning, but delegation and experience mean that we now have it down to a fine art. I would say the most important – and sometimes the most challenging – part of the process is securing excellent guest speakers. At the Trust, we start doing this sooner rather than later and have been lucky to secure some fantastically inspirational individuals to come to our past conferences. (I attach programmes to give you a sense of variety amongst our speakers towards the end of the chapter). As it is a student leadership conference, we always encourage our students to take the lead on it, and the day is interspersed with speeches and workshops conducted by students – and supervised by staff. We tend to ask our speakers to inspire our young people with their journeys, the hurdles they came across and ways in which they overcame them, and above all, a sense of what leadership means to them.

Parallel workshops conducted by students range from team building, public speaking, event planning, having difficult conversations, risk-taking, etc. All the skills taught in these workshops prepare and equip our young leaders for the future, in an enabling and exciting setting. The workshops are a mix of discussions and activities, and students have autonomy over the ones they wish to sign up for. The Sixth Form Executive lead the workshops, which last about 20 minutes each.

The conference tends to include opportunities to network with individuals from the world of work during breaks and lunches and this aspect of the day proves to be exceptionally successful. We throw in refreshments and a light lunch to give students a chance to experience what a 'real' conference feels like. The conference culminates with a survey for all students, which we encourage them to fill out there and then in order to help us gauge the value the event has had for students. A copy of the survey is shared below to give you a sense of what we ask:

An example of what our programme looks like is shared below:

Survey

Name and Tutor Group – (Encouraged but optional) _____

	Strongly agree	Agree	Disagree	Strongly disagree
I have enjoyed the conference and I am glad to have been invited				

I found the speakers engaging and inspirational				
The Ethos Team have organised a valuable and powerful event				
I would like to be invited to similar events in the future				

Further Comments about what you particularly enjoyed: _____

_____

_____

_____

_____

_____

Third Student Leadership Conference 2022
St Birinus School
International Men's Day
Monday 21st November 9:15 am to 12:30 pm

9:15	Welcome our Speakers at Reception/Students line up on top field and enter Hall in silence
9:20	Music
9:25	**Dr Khan to Open Conference**
9:30	**Address from Mr Manning**
9:35	HC1 to introduce Major Richard Grimsdell MBE
9:35–10:05	**Major Richard Grimsdell MBE**

Turnover Time: Students to discuss/make notes about what they have listened to/ come up with questions (5 minutes)

10:10	HC2 to introduce Mr James Atkins, full time professional wrestler
10:10–10:30	**Mr James Atkins**

Turnover Time: Students to discuss/make notes about what they have listened to/ come up with questions (5 minutes)

10:40	HC3 to introduce Mr Damian Hosen, Design Director at Sumo Digital (previously Creative Director at PlayStation)
10:40–11:00	**Mr Damian Hosen**
11:00–11:15	(Break and refreshments)
11:15–11:30	**Student Activity** *15 minutes*
11:30	AHB to introduce Mr Richard Kingscote, British jockey and winner of 2022 Epsom Derby
11:30–11:50	**Mr Richard Kingscote**
12:00	AHB to introduce Samantha Warnes, Director, Works Council Relations
12:00–12:15	**Samantha Warnes**
12:15–12:30	Q&A

Head Student to close conference/Vote of thanks

Anti-Bullying Week

Anti-Bullying Week, marked each November in the UK, is a significant aspect of the ethos calendar at the Trust. This is not so much because bullying is a major concern in our schools (it's not and we are most thankful) but more because a preventative approach to bullying and a mature awareness around it seems most wise. While we talk about values in connection with bullying through the year, a full week's focus has lasting positive effects. The preamble to Anti-Bullying Week is important as it is during this build-up that we reinforce just how significant the subject is. The build-up allows us to introduce the year's particular theme (determined nationally) and advertise the various events planned. The student leadership team are excellent at doing this and visit tutor groups on a rota to spread the word. Next, it is a question of ensuring that all events and activities are planned meticulously and quality assured. Central to our marking of Anti-Bullying Week is our 'Anti-Bullying Roundtable'. We select a specific group of approximately 25 students to attend this roundtable; in the past years, it has tended to be Ethos Leaders and Deputy House Captains from Year 10. The event is hosted in our conference room and chaired by a different member of staff each year (providing an excellent leadership opportunity for newly qualified teachers). The morning is spent in an open and honest discussion about the various complex facets of bullying, facilitated by the Chair. The Chair would have also created an agenda for discussion points in advance and is responsible for ensuring that the discussion is balanced and respectful. The ideas, issues, and solutions that emerge from the session are then shared more widely with the senior leadership team and eventually with the student body. It's a brilliant opportunity to step back and look at the bigger picture about bullying and is without fail an enlightening experience for those of us who run it. Student voice is like gold dust when it comes to pastoral and social aspects of school life.

Anti-Bullying Week also includes a popular chalk-in on different vast and open spaces around school, where, under supervision, students are encouraged to come out and add a supportive message on the school grounds. Yes, there is some theatre in the event, but the visual impact of the incredible and creative messages students contribute is stunning. There is nothing quite like standing on the second floor of the Humanities building and looking down on a sea of messages young people have written in support of 'anti-bullying'. It is symbolic of a stand they have taken. It's obvious, it's willingly done, and it's a powerful message to the community: we never have or ever will tolerate bullying in any form.

In addition, through the week, there are poster competitions for lower school, drama workshops for upper school, pledges for students (which are shared on social media and the school websites), odd socks day as well as rock painting and hiding, in the hope that it is found and re-hidden to keep the message about kindness in constant circulation. At the Trust, we believe that all students matter, and every individual has a right to be treated with kindness and respect. Weeks such as the Anti-Bullying Week enable us to revisit our values in depth and spread our message loudly and clearly. The approach is almost entirely preventative and the hundreds of students who get involved have taken the lead on deepening their values as young leaders.

House Captains in the Study Cafe

Wellbeing & Community Leaders

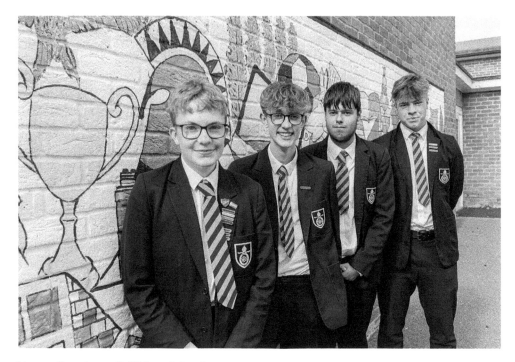

House Captains at St Birinus School

Mental health awareness week

The mental health and well-being of our students is never far from the fore of our minds – More so now than ever before. When global awareness weeks such as the Mental Health Awareness Week comes up, we as schools are presented with an opportunity to highlight our focus on this crucial part of school life. For us, this has always been a good time to invite external expert agencies to come and work with small groups or even entire year groups, depending on needs and circumstances. This is also an excellent opportunity to delve into the different facets of mental health. To this end, I have regularly invited nutritional therapists to come and speak to students about the inextricable links between well-being, nutrition, eating patterns, and physical exercise. Our visiting speakers have always handled this subject with great sensitivity and their advice has always been practical, wholesome, and compassionate. It is definitely worth having a detailed conversation with our speakers beforehand to give them the contacts off the group they will be addressing.

Furthermore, Mental Health Awareness Week presents an opportunity for subject teachers and heads of department to explore the ways in which their lessons might address this important topic. Art and photography department for instance are in a wonderful position to link their subject with mental health awareness. Be it a workshop, competition, or just an opportunity to bask in the sun for an hour with some paints and a small canvas (my favourite 'enrichment' activity) – students crave a variation from the norm and the impact of indulging in a mindful activity for a short period of time is enormous. At the Trust, we have offered a range of activities within the week, including a relaxation retreat with yoga after school, a workshop by a company that explores mental health through Shakespeare for Year 10, talks on body acceptance, and a welding carousel day which involves outside agencies as well as the county police, school health nurse, and school counsellors.

Pride Month

One incredibly important and positive step we took at the Trust recently was the setting up of clubs for members of the school's LGBTQ+ community and allies (which we all are!). We have a Rainbow Club and a Community Club who meet once a week and take the lead in planning for events such as LGBTQ+ Month or Pride Month. From a comprehensive survey I conducted with our student body, one of the things that became apparent was that our LGBTQ+ community would like to collaborate in the designing of any activities that relate to promoting the rights of the community or challenge homophobia. Here, I am sharing a structure of events created by these clubs to mark Pride Month in 2022. Members of the club are determined not to do anything that feels akin to ticking a box and invested a lot of time and energy, along with two dedicated staff members to mark this month meaningfully and beautifully.

Week	Event	Details
Week 1	Art Workshop	Students are invited to the Art Studio to spend an hour finding creative ways to express identity and solidarity through art
Week 2	Assembly	An introduction to Pride Month; why it is marked and what it means to be an ally. Each form is invited to come up with a pledge on inclusivity
Week 3	School Display	Students come together to create a display of the pledges and artwork they have created; the result to look like a giant LGBTQ+ flag
Week 4	Chalk-in and Cake Sale	Students to bring in Pride themed cakes which will be judged for winners; School Council to sell these cakes for charity later. A chalk-in at lunchtime to write messages of love and solidarity
Week 5	Pride Conga	Students bring in a coloured t-shirt to put on over uniform and meet on the field for giant conga with music. Pride flags/badges also for sale. Students could make banners ahead of this.
All month	Library	Books featuring LGBTQ+ characters or storylines on display in the library

To sum up, wherever you might be on your school's ethos journey, having a clear sense of what makes it on your ethos calendar and who is responsible for each of these events, lends a powerful structure to the way school culture is sustained. We will all have events, global awareness days, and moments of national and international significance that we will wish to privilege through the year. The readier we are for these, the better. And of course, what a fantastic opportunity to get creative about ways to engage the student body while delivering leadership skills along the way!

Tool kit

- Invest time in creating a structured and strategic ethos events calendar
- While some events will be pre-plotted, be prepared to be responsive to local and international affairs
- Place diversity and inclusivity at the heart of your planning
- Create a mixture of staff-, student-, and community-led events
- Invite guest speakers regularly and aim for a range of personality to be as inclusive as possible
- When handling challenging or sensitive subject matters, enlist the support of senior staff

The power of assemblies

Read on: to understand how assemblies can be game changers in sustaining a positive school culture. This chapter is packed with tips and suggestions to deliver excellent, empowering, and engaging assemblies consistently.

Assemblies are one of the most powerful educational tools available to us every day, each week, throughout the school year. A successful assembly is like gold dust: I always view these 20-minutes in the morning as a real opportunity to make a difference to a young person's day, potentially their week and possibly even their year. Off all my duties at school I regard planning an assembly as a right up there with one of the most important things that we can do for our young people. When we look back at the etymology of the word 'assembly' it is a gathering of a significant number of people, for a specific purpose. For centuries assemblies have been regarded as gatherings of utmost importance, defined by a purpose. To run an assembly is privilege that inspires me to think very carefully about what to say and how best to say it. Primarily, it poses an opportunity to capture the ethos of the school in a few powerful moments. It is also an opportunity to teach, so that students can leave the hall feeling good in the knowledge that they have learnt something. If things have gone to plan, they will walk away with the spark of curiosity ignited within them and inspired to dream the impossible.

When it comes to assemblies, we can all do better. We need to train our staff more regularly and more rigorously so that as a team we become accustomed to delivering assemblies that are engaging, powerful, meaningful, and enjoyable. All respectable schools and colleges gather student voice on a regular basis and this is an ideal subject to accumulate pupils' views on: what style of assembly do they enjoy, which topics and subjects are important to them and how do they perceive their own roles in an assembly? For school leaders, it is worth starting out by envisioning a biting cold morning in January (depending of course on which side of the hemisphere you might be reading this!), with our students lining up outside a large and equally cold assembly hall; quite possibly students will sit on the floor for the next 20 minutes, depending on numbers, facilities, and time. What can we say to them as leaders that could be worthwhile in this situation? How can we present to them in these 20-minutes to suggest loudly and clearly that we know their time with us is valuable? When it comes to assemblies, we need to consider content and delivery in equal measure, as the absence of either will result in an average assembly at best. Students' interests can be unpredictable and short-lived and no one knows this better than a teacher. It falls upon us to be armed with all the tools in our toolkit to deliver an assembly that young people will appreciate.

Throughout the school year I plan assemblies in a two-pronged way: one way is to plan assemblies in advance with global awareness days and pre-determined themes in mind. The other way is to plan assemblies responsively; at such times we respond to a local, national, or global situation that may have arisen and needs attention straight away. I don't believe that it is sensible or advisable to leave it to students to understand and explain complex global situations, which can be politically, culturally, and emotionally complex, to each other. I regard this is very much our responsibility as school leaders. Later on in this chapter I will say more about the sorts of assemblies I have planned responsively to situations, some with very short notice, even overnight, to prevent students feeling too worried or anxious about something that may have developed and needs to be unpacked by a figure of trust. Of course, part of planning and delivering assemblies on delicate subjects that can prove challenging, is to do a lot of careful thinking about maintaining our own neutrality as a school.

Let's start by talking about assemblies that are pre-planned and embedded into the school's ethos calendar right from the get-go. My approach is to pick out global awareness days, weeks, and months carefully to suit the ethos of our school, and then plan assemblies around these days. If we are marking a week such as Anti-Bullying week in the UK, then a useful strategy is to plan and deliver the assembly early on in the week, usually on a Monday morning, to launch the week's activities and tell students in detail about the plans we have and how they can get involved. Bookending the week with an assembly on Friday provides an opportunity to culminate the week's events with celebration and the marking stand-out moments, and distributing certificates, house-points etc. As often as possible, I invite students to help me deliver these assemblies and increasingly I have asked students to take the lead on them – but it is understandable if it takes time and practise to reach this stage. It is best to start with small steps by asking a student to be responsible for sharing a couple of ideas or a few slides before they take on something more challenging.

My top tips for brilliant assemblies

When planning powerful assemblies there a few key things that have helped me hone my skill, as well as those of my colleagues and student leaders:

Tip 1: Always plan with your audience carefully in mind. If your audience comprises Year 7 and 8, then remember you are dealing with 12- to 14-year-olds and you need to plan both your content and style accordingly. If this is the case, I would consider rephrasing and reiterating important ideas judiciously and privileging simplicity of style and delivery for maximum accessibility. Simplicity does not have to be tantamount to 'dumbing down' – it is more to do with conveying an idea with crystal clarity and crispness, free of unnecessary jargon or cushioning. Use examples they can identify with and let them know that their voices and opinions matter to you, ideally offering clear channels of feedback.

Tip 2: I regularly start my assemblies with a personal anecdote. There is a very simple yet profound reason behind this: as human beings we have evolved to respond exceptionally well to storytelling. The moment you tell your audience that you have something to share with them, either about yourself or about someone you know, perhaps an experience you've had, or something interesting you have witnessed, they are bound to sit up and listen. The lesson here is that to engage students with your assembly straight away, try to make it personal and heartfelt – prove to them with your words that the topic actually means something to you and that you are sharing the content with them with genuine warmth and sincerity. It is human instinct to respond with interest to any speech that starts with "There is something I wish to share about my life with you" or "It is hard to believe what I experienced a few years ago".

Tip 3: I have only just mentioned warmth but this is worth revisiting straight away. My experience is that that a speaker who delivers their words with unaffected warmth and passion establishes a very palpable (and wonderful!) connection with their audience. Such a speaker is far more likely to capture their listeners' attention quickly and sustainably than one who is distant or held back. In the physical space between a speaker and their audience there should exist no awkwardness – no barriers. However, this may well be a case of 'easier said than achieved' as how is this genuine warmth to be created? If we are indeed creating warmth by design then does it run the danger of becoming contrived? Can it be something that we can deliberately infuse it into our style? I would say yes. The warmth and genuineness in our manner, when it comes to speaking in public to hundreds of people, is directly correlated to how strongly we feel about the content we have created. A note on content: it is essential that this content is created by us and that we are not, at least in the main, delivering something that has been created by a colleague or lifted from the internet. The rest of the warmth will follow through our body language, how relaxed we appear, the amount of eye contact we're making and with how many people, and how we create our pauses and stops etc. I would go so far as to say that if I am feeling anxious or nervous before in assembly I tend to embrace those feelings as to me they now indicate purely one thing: how much I care both about my subject matter and about my audience. The absence of any nerves or anxiety could indicate a sense of detachment or indifference, although it is understandable of course that as a seasoned speaker nerves become less of an issue the more we speak.

Tip 4: never underestimate the value and power of adding humour to your assemblies when the occasion presents itself. When the occasion permits, don't shy away from a relaxed, more light hearted style; even when the jokes we make are 'cringe' (have you ever known a non-word to be so used so frequently?), students do warm to us when we make them anyway! My sense of humour tends to be on the drier side, often self-deprecating. Students who know me well enjoy it and look forward to it. There will be situations in which humour is either inappropriate or undesirable, and in these times, authenticity and warmth may well be the answer. At other times, it might be firmness that is needed – yet, even while being firm we can convey to our students that we care. Ultimately, that is what young people – all people! – need and want: to know that they are being looked out for and cared for.

Tip 5: Remember that assemblies by their very nature are a social gathering of people; we don't want our listeners to not participate at any point during the 15 to 20 minutes that we are addressing them. This would be hard enough the staff to do, leave alone young people. It is always possible to think of creative and empowering ways to engage our listeners into an assembly. Some examples might include asking for a show of hands, asking for participation from students who feel confident enough to do so, splitting students into groups on the spot, asking students to present with you to break up the monotony of any assembly.

Tip 6: It is worth agonising over how we use audio visual technology and resources in our assemblies. If you are using a PowerPoint, and chances are that you will, try to ensure that your slides are as minimalistic as possible. From experience, a visual stimulus on a projector with the bare minimum of words is often the best way to go. Not only does this take away from the struggle trying to read words from a distance for many students, it has the added benefit of creating intrigue. Some of the best talks in assembly that I have attended have been a series of pictorial slides, which the speaker expands upon as they move through that presentation or assembly. Font, background, colours, and design all make a significant difference to the impact of your assembly. The use of pastel colours from my experience has always been the best decision to make when it comes to designing an assembly PowerPoint, however this will not be the case for everyone. My message primarily is to invite you to consider design elements carefully when preparing and assembly

Tip 7: In recent years, I have started to think a little bit more carefully about how students enter the assembly hall. While this might appear to be a minor point, planning the entry could change the dynamics of your entire assembly. Sometimes, depending on the wider theme of the assembly, I use music as students come in. This could be in the form of something popular and catchy or a piece sung or played by a fellow student. Music puts a spring in our step and is such a quick and easy way to add a little pizzazz to our assemblies.

Tip 8: Don't be afraid of aiming to have ambitious content in your assemblies. Even if you have any fears or hesitation about how much of this content will be accessed and by how many pupils, I have notice that pitching high is always worthwhile. Even if there are students who find the content or the vocabulary difficult to access, remember that they will have left the assembly having learnt something new. If we are adding to the knowledge and experience of our students in any way, we know we are on the right track.

My hope is that some of these tips will lead senior leaders and teachers to think about their assemblies in a more dynamic way. I strongly believe that a whole range of teaching and non-teaching staff should take the lead on assemblies, sharing their voices and allowing young people to see them in a different setting and under a different light.

In his book *A School built on Ethos*, Head Teacher James Handscombe focuses almost exclusively on how assemblies contribute to the ethos and culture of a school. One observation that he makes in the book is about the idea that assemblies are not standalone events, and as such should not be viewed as a presentation. This will invariably result in assemblies feeling bitty and unrelated; Instead Handscombe suggest that assemblies should be designed to be part of a larger collective or ethos of the school if you like. He writes:

*When approached as a standalone presentation, however, even a truly brilliant assembly will lack power. An assembly's greatness comes from its place in a collection, which is why I believe assembly givers should also be listeners, and why the best cultural reference for an assembly is another assembly – ideally one given by someone else. These cross-references allow assemblies to reinforce and build on each other. They turn ephemeral, individual pieces into a rich and evolving tapestry of shared understanding. **They can tap into and develop the ethos of the school, and turn a building into a community** (Handscombe, 2021).*

Assemblies are the perfect time and place to impart cultural capital to our young people in a researched and wholesome way. As school leaders we can sometimes worry about how much of this will the received and absorbed, however, in my experience even if a cultural reference is not fully understood or appreciated, it can spark curiosity at some level and this in itself is a significant win. When it comes to cultural capital, we are all arriving at it from a different vantage point. My passion for literature, specifically post-colonial literature, will be unique and without doubt different from a colleague who may have a long-standing interest in Greek mythology, Islamic art and architecture, mathematical conundrums, European history, mountains and lakes, languages – this list could go on. For this reason it is important that we have a variety of staff members and school leaders planning and delivering assemblies. What each individual will bring to that assembly hall will be unique and remarkable and it is important to fully utilise the expertise that is available to us in-house. A few years ago I invited a colleague who had a tremendous passion for football, in particular Liverpool Football Club, to lead an assembly on the leadership skills that were involved in Liverpool winning the Premier League that year. Like many other schools, we tend to talk to our students about leadership very regularly; however there was something distinct and compelling about listening to a Maths and Computer Science teacher addressing a common topic in an unusual and exciting way. Our students wholeheartedly agreed!

Ask students

To benefit from pupil voice, which is always invaluable, I regularly conduct surveys inviting students to reflect on assemblies they have enjoyed as well as the ones that have been less popular. The surveys ask more detailed questions about features of assemblies students tend to appreciate and also left room for suggestions in the future. The results of these surveys only confirm what we as educators know to be true: young people are not naturally inclined to enjoy or look forward to assemblies, unless they offer something slightly special in content, style, or theme. The notion that many schools (including several I have attended or worked at) continue to deliver largely utilitarian and often rather mundane assemblies despite knowing student preference is worth probing. Do school staff require more training in oracy and public speaking? Do we need to upskill Heads of Year so that their assemblies are more dynamic and gripping? Is it beneficial, from time to time, to hold an assembly on an unexpected topic, while ensuring it is of value and interest? A good first step would be to start asking ourselves these questions.

At the Trust, we aim to offer a host of eclectic dynamic assemblies. While it is impossible to give a full picture, as assemblies are flexible and responsive to how events unfold, here is a snapshot of some assemblies that we have delivered year on year in our schools:

- International Woman's Day
- International Men's Day
- Modern Masculinity
- International Day of the girl
- Black History Month
- Pride Month
- LGBTQ+ History Month
- Holocaust Memorial Day
- Anti-Bullying Week
- Disability Awareness

- Eid

- Diwali

- Chinese New Year

- Remembrance

- Mental Health Awareness

- Autism Awareness

- Dyslexia Awareness

- Assemblies on Leadership: what it isn't!

- Assemblies about local and global charities

- Assemblies on Wellbeing, with a focus on what we can do to help ourselves

- Assemblies on Equality, Diversity & Inclusion

In addition, over the course of the past few years, I have planned and delivered assemblies in response to situations around us, as and when they unfold. These have ranged from the Russian invasion of Ukraine, the banning of schooling for girls in Afghanistan, Black Lives Matter, the conflict in Israel and Palestine, the controversies around the FIFA World Cup in Qatar (2022) – to give just a few examples. As schools we know that we need to maintain political and ideological neutrality, and in my experience, the best approach is to provide students with *the facts* in a way that is clear and engaging. Part of nurturing young leaders is giving them the opportunity to analyse sensitive situations and discover where they stand and how their values align. We need not shy away from opening up difficult topics so long as we have done the thinking and planning carefully. One way to approach more challenging assemblies is to ask ourselves how the most vulnerable students in our audience might feel, and plan to be inclusive of them. Using photographs, snippets from a range of newspapers, invoking various sources (including social media), allowing short periods of reflection time and exploring the nuances of the subject all contribute to sensitively planned and presented assemblies.

A good assembly, well planned and engagingly delivered, is game-changing; the best part is that unlike other aspects of ethos and culture which take time and patience, assemblies can be improved almost immediately and have impact without delay.

Tool kit

- Assemblies are gold dust: we must them wisely

- Plan assemblies to engage young people from start to finish

- Expose young people to a variety of styles, voices, and perspectives

- Experiment with interactive assemblies

- Create opportunities for students to present but train them well first

- Upskill staff to present powerful assemblies regularly

- Cover a host of different topics, some pre-planned and others responsively as needed

Young people, anxiety, and leadership

Read on to: find out more about the intrinsic link between our approaches to anxiety in young people and their investment in school ethos and wider school life. Discover ways to understand and address the anxiety students may experience generally and more specifically about leadership.

I am not a therapist, though I have been prone to offer well intentioned, albeit sometimes unsolicited, advice to anyone willing to listen. I thought I will get that clarification out of the way quite quickly! Despite my lack of qualifications in therapy however, I believe strongly that this chapter has a place in a book about young leadership. I believe this not just because fears around anxiety hold millions of young people back from achieving their full potential but also because I genuinely believe anxiety can be empowering. I don't make this statement lightly and must clarify that I speak as an experienced, longstanding friend of anxiety – sometimes this life experience makes us very valuable therapists – of sorts.

Anxiety can feel immensely isolating. You know exactly what I am talking about if you have experienced this loneliness first-hand. When in the throes of an anxious spell, with recurrent panic attacks, insomnia, low mood, and frustration as a result of all of the above, we can feel very alone. Surely, no one else is feeling quite so desperate, we might think. Surely, others don't worry as much about just setting out of the door and walking to the bus stop? Surely no one else has been up the entire night worrying about a speech they have to make in class or an exam they must take the next day. These assumptions are very natural when anxiety sets in. They regularly result in school refusal, episodes of panic in lessons, social discomfort, and a propensity to further isolate oneself. For someone between the ages of 11

DOI: 10.4324/9781003275985-10

and 18 the experience is likely to be exacerbated by issues such as peer pressure, hormonal changes and perhaps a reluctance to seek help.

Every year we are faced with a situation where a significant minority of students unconditionally refuse to partake in our leadership programme. The commonest reasons identified are the fear of public speaking, of being in the limelight and of course impostor syndrome – "I don't deserve to be a leader; who could possibly accept me as a leader when I can't?" There can be a profound sense of UN-belonging. We can't ignore this. Letting our anxious students sit and watch from the benches is the easiest option but easing them back into the playground is undoubtedly the most rewarding.

Schools have a number of useful strategies that all have a place in alleviating anxiety and improving the mental health and wellbeing of our young people. However, given the sheer scale at which we function, particularly in oversubscribed state schools, the approach is generic and sometimes procedural. Pamphlets, links to useful websites, physical fitness facilities, sessions with school counsellors, mentoring and a strong pastoral support system all make an enormous difference; however, despite these provisions, we are witnessing a spike in anxiety amongst students around the country, and indeed globally.

Here are some tried and tested approaches that have worked with my students, and tend not to appear regularly on leaflets containing (often reductive) advice on how to approach anxiety and low mood in young people:

- Without hesitation the first strategy on my list is to equip students with the knowledge that anxiety is absolutely normal. There is no one on the planet who has not experienced anxiety at some point or other, but what makes anxiety an 'issue' for people is its unsolicited arrival, when there is really no need for it, and its persistence for long periods of time. The symptoms caused by anxiety are perfectly normal too, though most people tend to fear the symptoms and wish them away, making the situation spiral out of control. There is solid science behind these chemical responses in our bodies, but what is important for now is to convey the normalcy of anxiety to our young people. This is a deceptively simple, yet extremely powerful first step.

- This may seem a little deep and philosophical, but our young people absolutely get it: talk to students about thoughts. We cannot do this all the time, but where the opportunity presents itself, it's worth reminding students that our thoughts must be distinguished from reality. It is so tempting to fall into the trap of "I have thought it so it must be true" that we regularly come across individuals who experience low self-esteem, low confidence, fear, and nervousness – all based on thoughts we have had. An awareness of our thoughts, not dissimilar to metacognition, empowers us to see thoughts for what they are – like pictures on a television screen that come and go. For me, this reminder is life changing.

- Make mindfulness a regular part of the daily routine: in her best-selling book *Why has Nobody Told me This Before*, Julie Smith compares mindfulness to 'driving lessons for the brain' (Shaw, n.d.). Mindfulness need not be overly complicated or drawn out, but a simple and regular practice does help a great deal with mood over time. A brain that is depressed is much more likely to spiral and become obsessive when rumination happens. Mindfulness and meditation help for this, at every age. We all need to update our knowledge on this and be equipped with tools when we need to come out of a dark or difficult space. Students can end up spending a lot of time ruminating on what they are not good at, rather than focussing on what they are in fact very good at; we have evolved to think the worst and let our thoughts run riot. The skill of awareness and just knowing when our minds are doing this can stabilise us. Moreover, as Smith suggests, "mindfulness is a state of mind that we can try to cultivate at any time" so for me it feels like walking around with a superpower that I can rely on to ground me. I think of mindfulness as awareness more than anything else and my students have become accustomed to me pointing out: "There you go – do you see that right there? That is you putting yourself down again. It won't help". Even if they don't change their actions as a result, just the fact that they become aware of their patterns is a huge part of personal growth.

- Physical activity must be part of every single school day: movement has powerful anti-depressant effects, generates more dopamine, and enhances our enjoyment of daily life. We are more likely to find joy when we are in this 'naturally high' state. The process need not be painful or complex in any way but exercise, as many of us know and can vouch for, can be absolutely joyous. Nature and the outdoors are scientifically proven to improve mood and enhance feelings of contentment and joy. As schools, we see students for such a large chunk of their day that we are well advised to make physical activity a regular part of each day; I know the benefits will be phenomenal.

- Human connection and shared experiences are an unbelievably powerful tool which we can and must make more off. They can cause our mood to shift and improve, provide comfort and alleviate painful thoughts. As schools we have the ability to create opportunities for young people to connect and engage meaningfully with others, and benefit from the shared experience. Low mood, depression and anxiety deceive us into wanting to be alone and withdraw ourselves from others, while what is actually needed is much the opposite: connection and relationships. Interactive assemblies, lunchtime clubs, group work, house meetings and event planning can all help to create these shared experiences.

  1 Practising Gratitude: Can range from big achievements or something smaller and seemingly less significant. We can train our minds to appreciate what is more positive. Perhaps just noting between one to five things in your day that

have felt good in some way (a delicious coffee, a conversation in the corridor, a chat at the bus stop, a compliment from a teacher, receiving house points, a treat in your lunch box – it is an endless list).

- Talk a lot about decision making: anxiety can make decision making extremely difficult, leaving us feeling confused and sometimes overwhelmed. A tendency to aim for perfectionism can exacerbate this anxiety and make decision making feel even harder. Here is where values can be so important, as they allow us to return to the core set and enable us to lift the fog and make a decision, no matter how small. As teachers, we have a lot more experience in the minefield that is decision making and are more trained to weigh the pros against the cons to ultimately move forward and make a decision. It is important we talk students through this in classrooms, in corridors and in assemblies. This modelling will slowly equip students with a lifelong skill, whether or not they are prone to anxiety and panic.

- Self-Criticism: some young people are prone to this from childhood, and it can be an extremely difficult habit to change quickly. As schools we will do well to talk more openly and regularly about the impact that positive self-talk and self-compassion can have in our lives. Activating our inner coaches and training our brains to become our biggest advocates makes us more emotionally self-sufficient. Ironically, we are so much better at doing this for others than we at doing it for ourselves. I have had to work hard to regularly give myself that figurative 'pat on the back' and having mastered (too strong perhaps!) the skill, I talk to my students about it often, getting them to actively look for the 'good stuff' within them.

- Healthy habits: This is a tricky one at secondary school level, where we cannot tell young people what to eat and drink and how to fuel their bodies, but we can make nutrition part of our narrative. This could happen through the pastoral team, the PE department, the PD department or indeed by outsourcing the expertise as we have done at the Trust. Secondary school is when students are seen to become more independent with their eating but also can begin to experience issues with body image, the reliance on caffeine and eating disorders. There is every chance that they are receiving all the right messages about healthy eating and nutrition at home, but can we afford to make this assumption for every student? Knowing as we do just how much nutrition is linked to mental health, mood and wellbeing, it does not make sense to remove this from the broader school narrative. I know that eating whole foods will be infinitely better for my mind than consuming processed 'junk', but each time I receive a reminder from someone I trust and look up to, I become more resolute in addressing this aspect of self-care.

● Emotional vocabulary: often, one we are feeling stressed, anxious, overwhelmed or sad it can become difficult define the right words to express exactly what is going through our minds. The resulting confusion can mean that we write off our emotional state utterly and completely. Adults routinely experience this frustration, so it is not difficult to imagine how challenging this might feel for many young people. In my personal experience both in my younger life and now, it has proved helpful to be able to associate my thoughts and feelings with a name or label. So instead of saying that "I feel rubbish" or "I am totally useless" I find it much more helpful to be specific: "I feel tired because I didn't get enough hours of sleep" or "I feel unprepared for an interview because I wasn't able to give it as much time as I would have liked" or "I feel unproductive as a result of having been home with a bad cold". School staff deal with challenging emotions every day, several times a day. It takes time and practise, but it is possible to equip a young people with the emotional vocabulary they need to express their emotions in a way that empowers them instead of paralysing them. The next time a young person approaches you, frustrated because "nothing" is going right in their lives, try breaking this down for them. Try unpacking the word "nothing". There is every likelihood that "nothing" refers to the student's struggle on that particular day, lack of sleep or a missed breakfast, with leaving the house late and being frazzled as a result or with planning an essay on a particularly difficult topic. Perhaps there is a deeper context here as well: conflict at home, hurtful communication from a friend or something difficult that has been unfolding on social media platforms. Often, when more than one frustration is at play, the young person quickly reaches a point why nothing feels right and all they want to do is shut down. Verbalising in concrete terms what "nothing" comprises is a healthy and mutually beneficial approach. In summary, we should use any opportunity we can to enhance our students' emotional literacy and equip them to use their voices effectively.

● Sleep and mood are inextricably linked: there is a bit of a 'chicken and egg' situation at play here as it can be hard to identify which comes first – lack of sleep or low mood, possibly triggered by something else. When I was 11, I remember my parents being called into school to have a meeting with my form tutor. The meeting, in its entirety, what about sleep. Or more accurately perhaps, about the lack of sleep that my teacher felt was seriously impeding my progress at school across all subjects. She wasn't wrong; as a child and later as a teenager I resented the idea of sleeping at night and saw it as a waste of a large segment of a 24-hour period (three children later, I can assure you I am of a different mind!). I would much rather read, write in my journal, or watch a film – and this is well before the option of using smart phones was on the horizon. With the entire world at our fingertips in one small machine that tends to stay very close to us when we sleep, can you imagine the reluctance to sleep that many teenagers experience now? According to Sleep Foundation, "prolonged sleep loss may negatively affect emotional development, increasing risks for interpersonal conflict as well as more serious mental health problems". The experts add that

> sleep deprivation can affect the development of the frontal lobe, a part of the brain that is critical to control impulsive behaviour. Not surprisingly, numerous studies have found that teens who don't get enough sleep are more likely to engage in high-risk behaviours like drunk driving, texting while driving, riding a bicycle without a helmet, and failing to use a seatbelt. Drug and alcohol use, smoking, risky sexual behaviour, fighting, and carrying a weapon have also been identified as more likely in teens who get too little sleep.

● We know these facts only too well, but need to find ways to reiterate the role of sleep on learning to our young people. I once made my entire Year 11 cohort listen to a Ted Talk on sleep and they went away feeling shocked by just how much it dictates how they might be feeling on any particular day. (Suni, 2000)

As schools we need to become so much better at providing young people with the toolkit they need to move towards the right direction in order to fulfil their goals. While we are not always in a position to do this in medical or psychiatric terms, everyday anxiety and low moods can definitely be addressed routinely, with a few positive steps. Just the provision of basic knowledge can make a difference, especially when it is provided in little chunks, often. None of this is about adding to our workload as teachers because that would be madness in its truest form; it is much more about redirecting some of our energy to nurture a happier and healthier community.

Anxiety and public speaking

My view on this may be the unpopular one, but I do believe that if someone absolutely does not want to speak publicly, such as in an assembly, they should not be forced to do so. That is not to say that we should not try our best to encourage students to do so and build their skills so that they are able to stand up and speak when they are ready, but I think it is both important and compassionate to say, "You don't have to this time. Let's wait till you feel ready". This reassurance, in my experience, takes an element of anxiety away yet leaves students with a curiosity about what they feel they can't achieve 'yet'. A student of mine, we will call her Zara, happened to be one of the most conscientious members of our student leadership team, but faced a mental block against public speaking. She would help plan assemblies, do all the leg work in events like conferences and talent shows, but when it came to walking up towards the stage, the anxiety was paralysing. So I decided to shift the focus from speaking in public, to just speaking. As schools, after all, one of the things we do best is live up to our moral imperative to help young people use their voices. To do this is the first important step towards getting our students to be heard, both privately in smaller settings and publicly to much larger audiences. More on how to create this culture for oracy in A Second Note: Finding your Voice.

Anxiety: the situation post lock-down

In February 2021 the BBC reported an unprecedented rise of 77% in children requiring specialised help for mental health conditions of a severe nature. For young people the absence of school, routine, socialising with friends, outdoor sports and an overall normalcy meant that stability and control Have been last. Countrywide, and undoubtedly worldwide, schools and colleges have seen an evident deterioration in both behaviour and mental health among young people. Schools are having to provide more counselling, provision such as exit cards and flexible workspaces to meet this unexpected need. Young people self-esteem and confidence seems to have taken a hard hit, with anxiety suddenly occurring in students who have no previous history of it. We have seen the rise of eating disorders, quite likely the result off young people controlling what they can't control i.e. food, and a fair of crowded spaces such as assembly halls, parades, and large-scale events. Along with several colleagues I picked up quite quickly on the deterioration in oracy post lock-down as well, which again is perfectly understandable after months of working behind screens. To remedy this wanted to things that we have done at the trust is to ramp up our focus on a oracy provision. You will find more on how to develop and deliver on oracy towards the end of the book. Additionally, I have found that it has been important to bring face to face enrichment and live wider school events back into the calendar as promptly as possible. School assemblies, House events, lunchtime in after school clubs, competitions and pair mentoring sessions all came back into action as soon as it was safe to do so. The strategies discussed above are all suitable an advisable to use in response to the anxiety students may feel in returning to wider school life post lock-down. Anxiety, especially social anxiety, can present a serious barrier against young people getting involved with co-curricular aspects of school life and months of lock-down has only exacerbated the issue. Fortunately, as educators there are several concrete steps we can take to lessen the impact of this anxiety.

Tool kit

- We need to address anxiety when we build young leadership skills

- Find ways to ensure our more anxious students feel like they belong to the leadership programme

- Keep anxiety a wholesome part of the narrative: find ways to 'normalise' anxious thoughts and feelings

- Encourage good habit forming (routine, sleep, nutrition, and exercise) to afford students the best opportunities for being mentally well

- Use existing systems to bolster student confidence and mood: peer mentoring, extra-curriculars, clubs, and house events

Ethos in the sixth form

Read on to: explore the ways in which ethos and young leadership can make a powerful impact in our 16–18 aged students, looking to prepare them to be socially responsible, independent, strong, and conscious leaders of the future. Learn more about the ways in which we can make young leadership provisions even more varied and dynamic at Sixth Form level of study.

It would not be amiss to ask why there is a need for a separate chapter on ethos within the Sixth Form. This is a valid question. In part the answer lies in our own journey as a Trust, where the Sixth Form was the final piece of the puzzle to fit into place and make our offer cutting edge. Our Sixth Form has been on a journey – an adventure if you like – whereby we have gone from being a provision that was satisfactory at best to offering an exceptional, enriched, and high-quality education to young people aged 16 to 18. While of course none of this happened overnight, it did happen over a relatively short span of time. As someone who witnessed the transformation, I can vouch that the progression of our Sixth Form ethos was palpable and exciting to track. This vantage point allows me to share the vision of the Sixth Form – and the concrete steps taken to realise that vision – with you. The second part of the answer as to why ethos at Sixth Form is worth addressing exclusively, is that I believe opportunities for enrichment and engagement with leadership should look different when young people get to this stage. My observation, echoed by many colleagues, is that something changes in that long summer after the GCSE examinations and before Sixth Form induction week. Our students return with an adult maturity and confidence – indeed even a greater understanding of their sense of self and identity. Leadership at this level should be distinctive and tailored to match this personal growth.

DOI: 10.4324/9781003275985-11

Before I delve any further however, a full disclosure: while I am very much involved in the ethos at the Sixth Form, the vision and strategy for this has been led
by my excellent colleague James Cross. I have watched his endeavours with interest and great admiration over the past few years, as he has navigated the Sixth Form
from a place where people attended primarily out of convenience and with apathy,
to a college of choice attended by young people from all over South Oxfordshire –
young people who take pride in their institution. Most of what I share with you in
this section is based on the work James has led, though of course I share this with
his gladly given blessing.

James' vision was to transform the existing Sixth Form into a serious place for
serious people; he hoped it would grow into a credible place of learning where
students have chosen to be for all the right reasons. An incredible amount of
groundwork was laid to ensure that it would be a Sixth Form with a rich and vibrant ethos alongside a culture for learning, in the hope that this rising tide would
take everyone with it. The narrative that grew very quickly was one of aspiration
and investment in the future of young people: students willingly embraced the
idea of creating a vision for themselves, equipped with the courage that they
could be who they wanted to be and that all doors were open to them, once they
had adopted the right attitude. Our conversations with these young people felt
different; the place just 'felt' different in a powerfully positive way. We had begun
to shift our ethos. We were changing the way we did things to ensure that values
were privileged above all else, and everything we did stemmed from these values. We were talking to young people about leading for legacy and ensured that
they all knew what this meant and entailed. Once students got on board with the
magic of leaving a place better than they found it, it felt like a switch had come
on. The Sixth Form staff team began to think of how they could expand their
ethos provision to make it better and much more inclusive. It was a question of
making wider student life an inextricable part of the fabric of the college.

The mission statement of the Sixth Form was one of the first things James approached. As I have said before, revisiting our mission statement is often the best
place to start as it allows us to ensure that we are aligned with our core principles.
James distilled his team's vision as such:

We aspire to become recognised across Oxfordshire as the Sixth Form of choice
for an exceptional education, and admired for our warm, welcoming climate and
respectful and ambitious culture. We aspire to shape future leaders who serve their
community and lead for legacy.

He goes on to explain that:

Didcot Sixth Form is…

a place where you come to learn and gain valuable qualifications

a place where you will be challenged to reach the destinations you desire and
supported to open as many doors as possible

a place to make lifelong friends

James adds that he makes no apologies for:

encouraging you to be the best version of yourself

insisting on respect and dignity between staff and peers

having (and holding you to) high expectations

He assures students that in return, they can expect:

committed, expert teachers

an organised, well-run Sixth Form

high levels of pastoral support

a wealth of opportunities

opportunities to lead and serve your community

to be listened to and taken seriously

This mission captures the vision for a culture that is both ambitious and respectful. Within this framework, James has found that the concept of leadership as service has gained a lot of traction among young people and James' own passion for serving the community has no doubt played a part here.

The next logical question is about how this vision for a cultural shift is put into practice every day. Here is a selection of some of the most powerful work done in the Sixth Form from an ethos perspective:

The leadership hour

The Leadership Hour is a mentoring and volunteering programme for all students at the Sixth Form, founded with the aim of making servant leadership systemic in the Sixth Form. In the first year off its inception the Leadership Hour so a 30% uptake from students; in the second year this moved up to 45%; the third year so 50% of students involved; this year we have over 70% of students partaking in the Leadership Hour and next year the provision will become mandatory for all students in the Sixth Form. The leadership hour offers a range of mentoring and volunteering opportunities, some of which include:

- Paired reading with younger students

- Literacy and numeracy work with students with special needs

- In class support at key stage 3

- Well-being checks with more vulnerable students (training is provided beforehand)

- Support with homework clubs after school

- Support with sports clubs during lunchtime and after school

- Support a student/group with a modern foreign language

- Providing 1-1 support for Y11 students doing GCSE Business next summer, focusing on exam technique and quantitative skills

- Presenting about global affairs in assemblies

- Planning and running school wide charity events

- Representing the trust at local community events

These roles are offered to all students at the start of the academic year and each position is accompanied by a brief 'job description'. The Literacy and Numeracy mentoring role, for instance, is described as such:

Mentoring vulnerable lower school students (Year 7/8/9) with their literacy, well-being, and key skills. High literacy skills are not essential, it can be seen as a 'journey together' to better understanding. Training is given on how to support their literacy, how to coach students and be a friendly face in school. In the past both mentors and mentees have found this extremely satisfying, forming warm relationships which have benefited both students. The mentoring is for one hour a week and the commitment must be made for the whole school year. Training is given during term one and mentoring will start in week 5. The mentoring session will be during one of your free periods.

These opportunities, when offered in a structured and meaningful way, contribute to our students' sense of self-worth and well-being as well the overall health of the community.

In addition to the Leadership Hour, all students in the Sixth Form are expected to be involved in a club or society through the 'Pivot Programme' – the umbrella term for all things linked to ethos and enrichment at the Sixth Form. The aim of the programme is to build confidence and character in an inclusive and enjoyable way. The Head of Ethos at Sixth Form explains that "The Pivot Programme focuses on servant leadership, critical thinking, creative problem solving, appreciating and understanding difference and... having fun!"

The pivot programme comprises

Visiting Speaker Series from inspiring individuals who have effected change. Over the past few years we have received visits from politicians (ex-Speaker of the Commons John Bercow), journalists (BBC Arts Editor Will Gompertz) and facilitated sessions on careers, finance, well-being, first aid, and personal safety.

Student-led Societies and Clubs (described below)

Qualifications: Extended Project Qualification, Oracy Society leading to a DSF certificate, Duke of Edinburgh Gold Award

Opportunities for leadership roles within the Sixth Form

Focus on servant leadership, ethical approaches and cultural values across the Sixth Form

Opportunities to explore creative problem solving, critical thinking and entrepreneurship through the Business Mentoring Programme and Careers Programme

Community – Activity – Service programme to strengthen perseverance, confidence, and self-awareness

Exciting trips to contextualise learning and broaden horizons

Below are just a few examples of the kinds of clubs and societies students can get involved with:

Finance Club is where students come to explore useful skills to help them become financial savvy.

LGBTQI+ tackles the big questions of gender and sexuality and is a safe place for all to explore who they are

Medical Sciences Society is for all who are interested in following this path at university.

Medical Sciences Society brings together those students looking to enter the worlds of science and medicine.

Oracy Society focusses on public speaking, following a termly programme that explores the spoken word and construction of argument.

Sports Club is open to those interested in recreational fitness

Yoga Club offers the opportunity for students to find their inner self and centre their mind and body

Art & Media Society seeks to explore the world of the Arts in all its forms, including pottery

Board Games Society offers students a chance to explore and play a host of board games, from the simple to the highly complex

Book club is for students who love to read and explore the eclectic world of literature

The Student Executive

The Student Executive is the final aspect of ethos at Sixth Form I wish to share with you. It is designed to replicate a university Student Union which "strives towards creating an inclusive and exciting atmosphere to enhance the school experience for all students within the Sixth Form and lower school". Serving as the 'voice' of the Sixth Form, The Student Executive is the foundation of progress and change advocated for students, by students. It is a space to share achievements and celebrate successes as well as dissect and unravel what is working less well. The Student Executive is made up of different sub groups: the head boy and head girl team, information, academic welfare, charity, environment, external affairs, ethos and sports. The idea is for the teams to work collaboratively and guide each other, while also serving as sounding boards. The Student Executive do not work in isolation but rather meet the rest of the Sixth Form student community regularly, in order to lead collectively as opposed to 'from the front'. There is always plenty of encouragement offered to the wider student community to step and take part without waiting for a leadership role or title. Together, this community of wonderful young people create an atmosphere of curiosity and aspiration, paving the way for rich and rewarding lives ahead – lives in which they know how to make a difference.

I spoke to James about how him and his team 'sell' this rich array of opportunities to students in the Sixth Form and he responded with just one word: 'culture'. Talking about culture as often as possible means that young people see it as an integral part of the fabric of our system, as opposed to something we privilege from time to time. James explained but he always invites prospective students carefully consider why they want to pay at this Sixth Form college – He added that they were a handful of young people who did in fact decide that this culture was not suited to them. Those who did decide to join, however, did so with a full and complete understanding of the ethos that they could expect. They began their Sixth Form journey aware of the culture of meaningful work and servant leadership that they would need to immerse themselves in. Within a few weeks of our new students joining us, this expectation becomes a matter of pride: they understand that their responsibility is to leave things better then how they found them. I also asked James about the character traits that he aspires to see growing within the student body and his response was refreshingly simple:

> Compassion. A non-judgmental view of the world. Knowing that if your idea of leadership leaves people behind then something is fundamentally wrong. Knowing that helping others helps you too. To be aware at the disadvantages that exist in the world and to play a part in addressing these. To walk towards difficulty instead of walking away. To do things but cause they're hard – that is the mark of good character. To be serious but not joyless. To be someone who doesn't walk away from a mess but rather helps to clear it up.

The icing on the cake is that students get involved with this ethos without the promise of any tangible rewards. At this stage of student life, the kudos of a badge or a certificate can wear thin – so the idea that intrinsic motivation is the prime reason for young people to get involved with leadership is most gratifying and promising (Figure 11.1).

Figure 11.1 Sixth Form Head Girl and Head Boy 2023–24.

Tool kit

- Return to your mission statement to ensure it aligns with your values

- Have a vision, no matter where you are on your journey

- Create diverse and meaningful leadership opportunities to match the maturity of students at the Sixth Form stage of their journeys

- Create a host of clubs and societies to keep students curious and engaged

- Encourage collaboration and a sense of leading for legacy

- Culture, Culture, Culture

Even younger leaders

Leadership at primary schools

Read on to: find out more about how the ethos of values-based leadership can be established and grown for much younger children in an engaging, enabling and inclusive way.

At the time of writing, there is very little by way of research or written material about student leadership at secondary school level. I can assure you that there was even less to be found on student leadership at primary school level. Leadership skills at primary level of schooling can feel like a complex and daunting concept to navigate; some might argue it isn't even a concept we necessarily need to consider at this stage of school life. I strongly believe that when it comes to leadership, it is never too early to start. I am a parent to a 14-, 11-, and 2.5-year old, all of whom engage with the concept of leadership every day. Often, their engagement with leadership happens on a subconscious level, without much thought or intention. Living with a toddler can be a most enlightening experience: he makes decisions throughout the day, decisions that enable him to shape his experiences in a way that he desires. I can't say that I have ever come across a type of person more self-willed and headstrong than a toddler – have you? I watch with fascination as he learns the skills of pleasing, manipulating, coaxing, sharing, and finding ways to let us know exactly how he feels and what he wants, when. Depending on the situation, he as his ways of showing kindness and gratitude, as well as anger, disappointment and frustration. Next summer, when he is three, he will be able to start attending our local school-based nursery, who will then have an important role to play in shaping his character, his identity and his relationship with other people. When we approach leadership as a set of values that we must understand, imbibe and live by, then it becomes clear that children at primary school level are absolutely ready for leadership. Drive, ambition, competition and the desire to succeed can come very naturally to children and our challenge is to hone and channel these traits, without compromising on their naturalness and spontaneity. At this young stage there is an

DOI: 10.4324/9781003275985-12

enviable independence off thought and freedom of speech, both of which we as educators can help to nurture and develop. At primary school level it is more important to "do leadership" rather than talk about it. In this chapter I offer suggestions about how we can create and nurture leadership when our students are very young.

Values-based leadership for children

Broadly speaking, I think primary schools do an excellent job of promoting values within their institutions. The primary schools I have visited, including the one my children attend, create visually appealing displays showcasing their values, address them regularly in assemblies, communicate them clearly to parents and ensure children are fully aware of their school values. Engaging meaningfully with values-based leadership will take this a step further by enabling children to live out these values while experiencing the first tastes of what it means to lead, and to lead well. Teaching children about leadership at this young age can involve a whole range of ideas, methods and activities. Group work is an excellent place to start – primary schools tend to a great deal of work during the day within small groups. This provides an opportunity to teach our children about sharing not just physical items but also ideas, views and feelings. As adults most of us seem to be better at speaking than we are at listening. In these important early years, we can make a significant impact on our children's abilities to listen to each other, to value and respect each other's opinions and beliefs. We need to be explicit about this expectation and nurture it consciously. Prevention is better than cure they say, and the more investment we can make in helping our children truly understand the school's values and demonstrate these in their behaviour towards each other, the greater the rewards later. Even within the framework of traditional styles of leadership we must afford opportunities two are more quiet and reflective children do engage with "being a leader" and "feeling like a leader". The sooner we can dismantle stereotypes about leaders looking, acting and talking in a certain way, the more likely we are to establish a strong and inclusive leadership culture. Group work also provides the opportunity to learn and practise the skills of negotiation; Young children are so accustomed to taking instructions from adults in the school setting that this experience is an invaluable part of their personal growth. It also encourages them to make decisions and voice them to other people, without worrying excessively about their reactions. While the immediate benefit of a group or team activity maybe to work on finishing a project or complete a piece of writing, as far as the bigger picture is concerned, children are learning teamwork, decision making, creative problem solving, resilience and trust – qualities fundamental to good leadership.

At primary school level we also have the opportunity to teach our children that leadership is first and foremost about leading ourselves – much before we think of leading others. It is a time for school leaders to think carefully and creatively about the ways in which this can be achieved: invite children to think about young leadership, lead by example, encourage wholesome communication, focus on self-awareness, self-belied and experience pride in what they accomplish. To remove the obsession with winning, what else can we do in the early years to make children see the value in the process and not just the final result? As adults most of us understand that good leadership is about taking others with us, listening well, showing compassion, and learning to rise when we fall, but it would be naïve to assume that all 'grown-ups' subscribe to this version of leadership. A quick glance at the world around us shows enough examples of toxic leadership, and the havoc wreaked by selfish leadership behaviours, to know that something is not quite right in the way leadership is approached across the board. I like talking to my own children about leadership being first a responsibility, then a privilege. Viewing leadership as a privilege beyond all else is problematic as it can result in egotistical thinking and behaviours. It is much healthier to think of being a leader as a chance to help others and improve systems rather than obsess with the title and any power it entails. Unfortunately, we cannot rely on the media in its current shape to teach our children about wholesome leadership, though this is beginning to change. It falls on schools and families to bring about an understanding of leadership as service and inculcate the desire to leave things better than we have found them.

Another important aspect of raising good leaders in the early years is to find ways to equip our children with a sense of the world around them and their position within it. As educators we have a strong instinct for what our children should be exposed to, and we do well to keep them shielded from many of the harrowing global stories that are splashed across our newspapers daily. However, if we don't find a way to talk to children about major local and international developments, we miss the opportunity for them to receive a reliable account of these situations from people they trust the most. A sense of the world around them, and how global events unfold, affords children the chance to form their own views and values and to begin to develop a sense of 'right' and 'wrong' which will stand them in good stead. It also encourages children to know that people around us look, talk, think and act in ways that might feel unfamiliar, but are equally valid and worthy of respect. I often talk about bringing the world into our schools being one of the best things we can do for the emotional and intellectual development of our young people.

Public speaking

Speaking in public can be a significant aspect of leadership at any level. Sometimes, we make the mistake of assuming that all leaders are versed in the art of public speaking, or that somehow this comes naturally to them. I believe there are two important things to bear in mind here:

One, we need to be intentional about teaching our children to communicate in public. Voice, tone, pace, body language, content, engagement and eye contact are not skills that families tend to deliberately teach at home and so it falls upon schools to do so consciously and regularly. My experience of early years education, many years ago and in a different country, was that of being given several opportunities to speak in public (parents love seeing their little people on stage after all) but without much guidance about how to do so effectively. It was only when I became a teacher that I witnessed a colleague conducting a lunchtime session with students about how to speak in public effectively that I really understood the impact this intentional training can have. Without it we are just assuming that if a child can speak, they can speak in public and hope that they will eventually improve. I like to talk to younger students about the five P's of public speaking:

Position: Consider how you stand and while your confidence is still building, plant yourself on the floor like a solid oak tree. Your roots are so firmly planted in the ground that nothing can shake you.

Power: Remember, in this moment you are powerful. You have the power to make people smile, laugh, reflect, learn and question. Knowing the effect of this power will help you perform your best.

Pride: The very fact that you have made the decision to speak in public is worth celebrating. Take pride in taking that first step and it will shine through your expression and your words.

Pace: For the next few minutes, while you are speaking, you belong in that space. You are entitled to this time and should feel no rush to finish and run off. People want to listen to what you have to say, and they want to absorb it so don't feel like you need to rush your words!

Present: Try to be present and enjoy the act of public speaking – I really wish someone had encouraged me to enjoy this rather than worry and lose sleep over how I might come across. After all, we are the best versions of ourselves when we are having a good time at the same time!

Creating leadership positions

Most primary schools I have been to have leadership positions available for children, be they in the form of classroom monitors, form captains, school councillors, house captains or library monitors. My work over the last few years has led me to become creative and think unilaterally about the way we engage young people with leadership position, and the first step to achieving this is to expand the ways in which we think about the positions we offer. The more variety we can create, the more eclectic our offer, the more the chances of being truly inclusive of the student body. When I attended school, being a house captain was unthinkable without having an impressive sporting background – this precluded me straight away. Prefects seemed to be elected through a popularity contest of sorts, which again meant I didn't quite make the cut. The Head Boy and Head Girl may as well have been called 'prom king and queen' (no lingering resentments of course) as there was never any mystery as to who would land in these much-coveted leadership roles. Even then I wondered where I fitted into this scheme of things. What leadership roles were available to someone who never missed a day of school, worked hard, was respectful and warm but did not necessarily create sparks everywhere she went? It turned out, in my experience, there were none. But who knows the wonders it would have done my self-esteem and confidence if I had indeed landed in one of those positions. It is a huge mistake to cater exclusively to our 'natural leaders' and leave the quiet ones to 'get on with things' because, presumably, that is what they are happiest doing. Here are some tangible suggestions about the sorts of leadership roles primary schools might consider offering, with a view to engaging students inclusively:

Community Leaders: who plan creatively for the wellbeing and growth of the community e.g. organise activities for Anti-Bullying Week and Remembrance Day

House captains: who plan house competitions, Sports Day, present house points updates in assemblies, drum up house spirit

Eco Team: who consider and plan for sustainable living measures (in collaboration with the catering, site and gardening team) and update the school community regularly on activities planned towards this aim. They may look at areas such as recycling, saving energy and reducing plastic as well as updating the school's social media and website with any new initiatives.

Diversity leaders: who promote cultural, ethnic and religious diversity by planning events around festivals such as Eid, Hanukah, Christmas, Chinese New Year, Diwali etc.

Lunch time leaders: who work along adults ensure that younger children are happy and content during lunchtime by offering to provide company, friendship or a helpful hand. They may organise lunchtime games, fundraise for new equipment and be responsible for putting equipment away at the end of lunchtime.

Well-being ambassadors: who work to enhance the wellbeing of the school community by planning events, creating displays, hosting cake sales and 'jazzing up' school assemblies and even lessons!

Music ambassadors: who promote all events and activities related to music and play instruments/sing in assemblies, after school events, award evenings etc

Librarians: who assist the Library Manager with the keeping the Library looking tidy and welcoming, reviewing books, hosting reading events and promoting a reading culture.

Digital Leaders: who are ambassadors for the school's digital strategy and offer support with all things related to technology and the benefits it can bring to our daily lives. They may also present assemblies and spread awareness about the dangers associated with social media and promote digital wellbeing.

This list of leadership roles can be as long and expansive as we would like it to: Student Councillors, Prefects, Assembly Monitors, Playground Leaders, Digital Leaders and Display Monitors are all wonderful roles to get even our quietest children involved. Our job is to ensure that there are meaningful job descriptions for all these roles and that students gain more than just a badge and glory from their positions.

Having thought hard about ways to promote meaningful leadership further within the primary school in our trust, a few years ago we decided to launch a Leadership Star Award for Years 5 and 6. While this award shares the same premise as the Leadership Ladder that we use in our secondary schools, we have modified it significantly be more suited to primary children and given it a unique and distinctive feel so that students don't arrive at secondary school expecting more of the same. Lisa Knight, a wonderful primary colleague who is Assistant Head Teacher at Sutton Courtenay Primary School was instrumental in devising this award, shared below (Figures 12.1 and 12.2).

The Sutton Courtenay 'Star' Award

Name:_____

Activity	Date	Signed
In School (Point 1 is compulsory then Select 4 more)		
1.Wear correct uniform consistently.		
2. Take responsibility for a class job for a term eg book monitor, PE trolley monitor		
3. Take part in a House Event, representing your house team positively.		
4. Be a reading buddy with younger children in school for 6 sessions.		
5. Lead a short learning activity eg a maths starter or topic quiz.		
6. Be a leader for one House Event, taking responsibility for a job to support the running of the event.		
7. Participate in leading part of an assembly in a group – eg read or perform a story.		
8. Apply for a job on takeover day.		
9. Support at the running of a Foscs or charity event held at school.		
At Home (Select 3)		
10. Take responsibility for a job in the home for 2 weeks eg: emptying dishwasher, putting washing away, clearing the table.		
11. Do a piece of additional research at home linked to a school topic to share.		
12. Catch a public bus to Didcot or Abingdon (asking for the ticket and giving the driver their fare)		
13. Help someone outside of your household (A family member or family friend) with a job eg gardening, washing car, putting bins out.		
Growth Mindset (Both)		
14. A new skill I have learned is …..		
15. A piece of work I work really hard on was…..		

Figure 12.1 The Sutton Courtenay 'Star' Award – Progress Card'.

The Sutton Courtenay 'Star' Award

(Your Home Copy which you can tick off to keep a check of what you need to do next)

Activity	Tick when Achieved
In School (Point 1 is compulsory then Select 4 more)	
1.Wear correct uniform consistently.	
2. Take responsibility for a class job for a term eg book monitor, PE trolley monitor	
3. Take part in a House Event, representing your house team positively.	
4. Be a reading buddy with younger children in school for 6 sessions.	
5. Lead a short learning activity eg a maths starter or topic quiz.	
6. Be a leader for one House Event, taking responsibility for a job to support the running of the event.	
7. Participate in leading part of an assembly in a group – eg read or perform a story.	
8. Apply for a job on takeover day.	
9. Support at the running of a Foscs or charity event held at school.	
At Home (Select 3)	
10. Take responsibility for a job in the home for 2 weeks eg: emptying dishwasher, putting washing away, clearing the table.	
11. Do a piece of additional research at home linked to a school topic to share.	
12. Catch a public bus to Didcot or Abingdon (asking for the ticket and giving the driver their fare)	
13. Help someone outside of your household (A family member or family friend) with a job eg gardening, washing car, putting bins out.	
Growth Mindset (Both)	
14. A new skill I have learned is	
15. A piece of work I work really hard on was.....	

In addition to this individual award, younger students participate in a broader class award, where they come together to earn points towards receiving their prize, and the accompanying glory!

The Sutton Courtenay Class Values Award

Are you......Ready, Respectful and Responsible?

During this school year, you need to work together as a class to achieve 8 of the challenges from the list.

Challenge!	Detail of how to achieve the Challenge	Achieved
1. Responsible for belongings	Be responsible for belongings - Keep the cloakroom tidy and ensure lunch boxes, reading folders and water bottles are in the correct place. This needs to be done consistently for at least a term.	
2. Class Display	Work together to produce work and create a display in the classroom or around school, sharing your learning.	
3. Perform poem or song	As a class learn a song or poem by heart and perform it in a Friday Star Assembly.	
4. House Event	Take part in a house event, supporting everyone to be involved. This could be a sporting event or quiz.	
5. Good Manners	Be recognised for demonstrating good manners consistently for a term. For example saying please and thank you, letting others though the door, behaving respectfully in assembly.	
6. Responsible for school pet	Plan and prepare to have our School Dog Cessie for a day or 2 mornings. What will she need? Where will she rest? Who will walk her?	
7. Class Trip	Plan and go on a class trip – Where will you go? What will you do? What do you need to take? How will you keep safe?	
8. Class Vote	Take part in a class election, understanding the reason for an election and the process. This could be for the School Council Representative or another class election.	
9. Class Assembly	Deliver a class assembly to the rest of school, sharing what you are learning about.	
10. Grounds Tidy	As a class, do a school grounds walk – pick up any play equipment left out, rubbish (gloves on) and make a list of any jobs that need doing.	
11. Share your learning	When as a class you have produced some work you are extremely proud of, ask another class for some time when you can share it with them. This might be stories you have written, art or models you have produced or even dances or pieces of music you have created.	
12. Growth Mindset	Identify an area of learning during the year which you know is going to be a challenge for you as a class. This will become your Growth Mindset Challenge, which you are going to demonstrate a positive 'can do' attitude for. You will have to work really hard and support each other to be able to achieve this.	

Each time you achieve a challenge, Mrs Knight will come and stamp it to show you have achieved it.

Once you have achieved 8, you will receive a Class Award and Class Reward Activity.

Figure 12.2 Here The Sutton Courtenay Class Values Award.

Embedding leadership opportunities in a variety of ways allows young children to develop a rich and meaningful understanding of school values and will encourage them to live by these values both in and outside school. Leadership in a broad an inclusive way also creates confidence and a sense of advocacy and belonging – belonging not just to the school community but to leadership as well. It goes a long way in reducing the gap between "those who can lead" and "those who can't lead". The blue sky thinking and the ability to form a vision which is so integral to school leaders is also important for our children to learn. It falls upon us to teach them to set goals and dream big. It is naïve to take for granted that all children are naturally optimistic and aspirational, nor is it realistic to assume that there social and family backgrounds nurture such thinking – as educators we can and must step in to make their worlds bigger and to invite them to be ambitious for themselves. Such an ethos, where values-based leadership is privileged also build the scale of strong communication and involvement within the community. We know all our children have a voice, but we also know that not all of them are equipped or encouraged to use it. Even at primary school level we need to be intentional in creating a culture where our children believe in the right to dream and the right to belong.

Tool kit

- Talk to our youngest students about leadership; it is never too early to start
- Make values come alive and develop a sense of leading with values
- Create exciting and meaningful leadership roles with specific job plans
- Actively teach public speaking skills, so that their confidence grows organically
- Encourage vision setting and dreaming 'big' at a young age

A note

Making the most of tutor time

This section is presented as 'a note' rather than a chapter; this is not because it was an after-thought – quite to the contrary – it is incredibly important but the message is brief and simple, hence a note.

The role of the tutor, and ways in which tutor time (no matter how brief) can be used for enhancing school life, student experience, opportunities for leadership, wellbeing, and ethos as a whole, is highly significant. This section of the book enables me to share tried and tested models for how each tutor time over the course of a week can be used in a structured and creative manner, drawing from examples I have seen and enjoyed in my career. The structure for tutor time over the course of the week is the combined effort of our dynamic Senior Leadership Team, but my particular thanks for sharing so generously with me goes to my colleague Adam Tamplin, Assistant Head Teacher for Standards and Culture.

Part of my role is to design thought provoking and easily deliverable ethos activities for students to enjoy at all stages of their school life; this most certainly has been a labour of love. In this chapter I share some of my best ideas, including how to encourage our young people to create vision boards, practice discussion and debate, become globally minded, explore fascinating career options, enhance their vocabulary, enjoy mindfulness, and cultivate their leadership skills. I also consider the role of the tutor when it comes to enhancing the wider school experience for each child, factoring in time constraints and teaching responsibilities and suggest ways in which tutors can maximise their impact on young people.

Tutors are almost always teachers too, and juggle this immensely important pastoral responsibility with a demanding teaching timetable. In my career so far, there have been schools that take this role as seriously as they have to: safeguarding, registering pupils, and delivering important notice to students. At the Trust, the tutor is a key role-player at the heart of the school: someone who can make a real difference every day. This doesn't happen overnight. It is a result of a strong vision for tutor time and committed investment in up-skilling all staff to deliver this role well.

DOI: 10.4324/9781003275985-13

One of the first steps we took at the Trust a few years ago was to extend tutor time from 15 to 30 minutes; this instantly made it feel substantial and allowed a range of stakeholders to provide resources to fill this time meaningfully. We provided training to our staff on how to conduct these sessions in an engaging, meaningful and time efficient way.

From an ethos perspective, my first advice to tutors was to reiterate the 'Why'; why we were doing any of the things we had planned for tutor time. Students often, and reliably enough, wonder 'Why bother?'. Why bother is a great place to start any sort of training or Continuing Professional Development (CPD) in my view and so when I talk to tutors at the start of each year, I tend to start with just this.

Why bother with delivering ethos sessions in tutor time?

Let's begin at the beginning with moral purpose. The beautiful thing about talking to teachers is that they are already fully convinced about the moral purpose behind what they do each day. Remind them that using tutor time to deliver a weekly ethos slot helps to nurture well rounded, globally aware, compassionate, and happy young people. Students will spend an entire day of anything between four and six lessons absorbing academic content and these first 30 minutes will be transformational if we use them wisely. I offer lots of suggestions as you read on.

These 30 minutes enable us to capture and convey school values in a tangible and coherent way. There is always the danger with school values becoming 'words, words, words' but a well-planned, engaging activity can help convey these values in a way that feels natural and organic, not didactic, or repetitive.

All successful schools devote a huge chunk of time and resources to wellbeing because we cannot overstate the importance of being highly intentional in our approach to it. Tutor Time is the perfect opportunity to inject some joy into a school day. There are a few weeks each year where one of our colleagues runs a 'House of Fun' Cup – essentially a varied and exciting virtual 'live' house quiz that is masterminded by Dr Mike Suggate, one of our most passionate and devoted Heads of House. To begin with this was a post-lockdown strategy to help regain normalcy at school but proved so popular that it is now an integral part of the school calendar.

In the past few years the weekly ethos slot has proved to be an invaluable safe to impart knowledge and explore challenging situations, locally or globally. As schools we have a duty to help young people make sense of the world when things don't naturally feel right – or when confusions arise as a result of myriad news sources, all reporting the same event differently. Recent examples where we have stepped in to offer a balanced and simplified (not simplistic) understanding in the Israel/Palestine conflict, the situation with girls' schooling in Afghanistan and the war in Ukraine. I believe schools should make this a priority. Listening to music, watching a scene from an uplifting Christmas film, playing Kahoot, making one-minute impromptu speeches – they all have a place when we aim to give students the best possible start to a day. One of our Year 8 students recently delivered an impromptu speech on "What came first: the chicken or the egg?", wowing all those in the tutor room with his clever use of science and logic and of course generating a whole lot of wholesome laughter. It's arguable that this did not directly add to anyone's learning, but for me the winning argument (by a landslide) is the contribution that morning's activity made to our students' wellbeing and state of mind through the day. An metaphorical breakfast if you like, that sets students up for a day's learning.

As schools we scramble for time to promote the house system and the competitions that take place through the year. Tutor Time is a great way keep the house system at the fore of students' minds and create that sense of healthy competition, particularly if your forms are grouped in houses. Creating banners for Sports Day, drumming up enthusiasm for an upcoming house event or devising house chants all count!

Tutor time enables us to touch upon aspects of school life that can have a positive effect on every single student. Lunchtime and after school clubs are fantastic, as are trips to exciting destinations and schools we should never be without these, but they come with an exclusivity. With the best intentions, we cannot guarantee that they will lead to enriching every student's wider school experience. This is where tutor time is gold dust: all students partake and benefit. It is our best shot at empowering young people in bite sized portions.

Tutors should feel equipped to convey the 'why' to students: expect students to be anything from curious to sceptical to downright indifferent. Tutors, hence, should be able articulate this with purpose and passion.

That's that for 'why bother?'

So 'how do we do it?'

Firstly, ensure that tutors have the resources they need in good time. Also ensure the resources are detailed enough so that while tutors can scan them in advance (in ten minutes or so), there is no expectation for them prepare anything. The resources can be prepared by one member of staff with responsibility for ethos (my colleague Paul and I divide and conquer at our schools), or there can be a rota involving different members of staff including Heads of Year, School Council Lead, Careers Lead, Wellbeing Officer etc. Recently, for instance, I have been able to share with tutors an ethos session designed by Nathan Rees, our Director of Computer Science and Digital Lead, on 'Safer Internet Day'. Similarly, Phil Mahoney, our Mandarin Lead, created some very engaging sessions on Chinese New Year. Our Student Exec in the Sixth Form are often put in charge of creating and delivering resources to younger students. The more voices we have, the better it is for our school community. Most recently, our Diversity Leaders, headed by Oliviya Edison, Chloe Cormack and Nathan Green (all just incredible individuals) launched our very first Culture Week. Culture Week entailed zooming in on different, exciting aspects of world cultures each week, from clothing and food to dance and music. Our Diversity Leaders created the resources, I quality assured them to ensure they were engaging, interactive and high quality. With all tutor groups enjoying these sessions simultaneously, the buzz we had around school is hard to capture in words. Some tutors naturally took this in a direction of their choice, watching clips and wearing props that students willingly contributed. Those who did not, were still able to offer their groups a rich and enriching experience. Our surveys post Culture Week show that that 100% of tutors felt that these sessions made a positive different to their students' school experience. Culture Week is of course just one example; having a close eye on the school's live ethos calendar is a solid starting point as it indicates what may be coming up from a school-wide, local, national, or global perspective and can dictate how best to create resources to fit in thematically.

More ideas for enrichment activities

- Ted Talks: we are spoiled for choice here. There are so many inspirational speakers and such a wide range of topics to choose from. I think of Ted Talks as our very effective 'cheats' guest speaker option!

- Create your own Ted Talk: this is just a newer and fresher approach to public speaking, whereby we ask students to prepare and deliver a brief talk on a subject of their choosing in a competition setting.

- Weekly quiz: a lot of schools have these in place, but if you don't, it is a great option to have in the bank as quizzes have a way of lifting the mood and energy in a classroom almost instantly.

- News updates: I sometimes create a rota in advance and ask students to present a section of the news each week. This is absolutely fascinating as students decide which aspect of the news they wish to privilege and gives me great insight into them as people. However, a more convenient approach might be to subscribe to an age appropriate and well rated news platform, ideally in audio-visual form.

- Explore a country or culture: if you have student Diversity Leaders, they can be asked to create a short an engaging presentation on a region or culture of their choice. Little nuggets of knowledge like these keep us outward facing and globally knowledgeable.

It would be amiss not to mention the success of mindfulness in tutor time, which has been rapidly gaining popularity around the UK. Those of you who bring a mindful practice to your daily lives will know that by teaching this, we teach a skill for life. We are truly empowering our students by making them more mindful and grounded in an age of distraction and raging digitalisation. With the escalation in stress, anxiety, and eating disorders in young people, no amount of excellent pedagogy will make a difference unless we are doing enough to mitigate the effects of growing mental health disorders. If there are students who are not convinced, they still have nothing to lose from trying it and for those on board, what a great start to the day once a week! There are videos, books, apps, and resources aplenty to enable us to make a start with this, as many schools already have. It is an area where research is very much ongoing but evidence so far suggests that small doses of mindfulness are beneficial at any age.

- Present a review on a book
- Watch a short film or documentary
- Mentoring from older students

Delivery and discussion

Sessions delivered in tutor time must be done so with purpose, as you would a lesson, except all the planning has been done and there is no marking involved! Students will respond with enthusiasm that mirrors the tutor's, so from experience, this needs to be a priority. Combining this engaging delivery with confidence and warmth makes the ethos session so much more powerful; the confidence will come from knowing the material well beforehand, so it is important to be a good few steps ahead of the students. When I was a tutor, I often encouraged keen students to lead on tutor time ethos sessions, which was rewarding in more than one way: I could reserve my energy for the rest of the day, monitor behaviour or have individual conversations with tutees while affording young people yet another opportunity to lead. This can be done via a predetermined rota, where students can expect to deliver a session in individually, in pairs or alongside the tutor. Another result to aim for is a lot of participation, which can be a combination of volunteering or cold calling – as long as it feels inclusive and a range of individuals are participating, it really doesn't matter what shapes this takes. It's a refreshing 30 minutes where structured pedagogy can be parked in favour of enthusiasm and spontaneity. Think-Pair-Share has always lent itself well to discussions when it comes to sensitive topics and avoids certain students from monopolising the session. Try and enjoy it yourselves – it's contagious!

Managing opinions and responses

Ethos can sometimes feel unchartered and vague territory, which can make it difficult to navigate. You can expect differences in opinion when discuss topics that are sensitive or generate heightened emotions; we are after all catering to a diverse body of young people with varying family backgrounds, beliefs, and opinions. As teachers we are good at establishing that while we are all entitled to an opinion, respect for each other is paramount and non-negotiable. The school values play an important role here as we can keep bringing it all back to our school values; they keep us grounded and allow us to explain why there are boundaries in place.

The cognitive diversity that students bring can feel difficult to control and manage but remember that ultimately it is enriching and powerful. Of course, tutors must pass on anything that stems from these sessions as a potential safeguarding concern but also have your own set of non-negotiables in place. Below I provide an example of what this might look like and it could be very worthwhile to create a charter for discussions as a class, so that the non-negotiables feel shared and unanimous.

- Ground Rules for Discussion

- Listen respectfully, without interrupting

- Listen actively and with an ear to understanding others' views

- Criticise ideas, not individuals

- Commit to learning/be open to difference

- Avoid blame, speculation, and inflammatory language

- Allow everyone the chance to speak

- Be inclusive in every way, including in the language we use

- Body language – know that this can hurt people

With a difficult question, should you feel uncomfortable answering it, be honest and say you will pass it on or come back to it. In my experience students appreciate this kind of honestly and also see teachers as 'normal' people. We don't know the answer to everything; it's best to be upfront about this!

What the week may look like

Having a structured, even regimented, approach to tutor time is a sensible way to organise these precious minutes of the day. We have 30 minutes, which feels luxurious, but I have worked in schools where we have had 10 or 15. Whatever your timetable allows, a structured approach will enable our young people to get the best possible start to the day they can.

Reading for pleasure

Reading for pleasure is another highly valuable and rewarding use of tutor time. Investing in class sets of fiction can be a very worthwhile step, though may not always be possible. It can be helpful to accompany this with either an audible subscription or a tutor reading out loud to students to get all our students on a level playing field as far as reading goes. It may take an entire term to complete a book but imagine the satisfaction at the end. You will have your keen readers in any group, but this is looking less the case when you look across the board. At the Trust, we have developed a reading strategy, led by our fabulous Library Manager Leoni Barnes, that allows us to work consistently on this aspect of student life where we

> recognise the value and importance of Reading for Pleasure, not only as a means of improving academic outcomes for students, but also as a skill which can have enormous benefits throughout life. Some of these benefits include: a broadened imagination; an increased vocabulary; improvements in the ability to concentrate; increased levels of empathy with others; and the ability to enjoy solitude.
>
> (www.didcotgirls.oxon.sch.uk, n.d.)

Reading has been called the "master skill of school, unlocking the academic curriculum for our pupils" by Alex Quigley in 'Closing the Reading Gap' (Quigley, 2020) According to data from 2019, 27% of primary school ages children did not reach the DfE's (Department of Education) expected reading level so it becomes incumbent upon us to help them grow as readers. In 2019, only 73% of pupils reading primary school reached the expected reading level. (Department for Education, 2019) In 2022 the OECD (2002) found that reading for pleasure played more of a role in long term success compared to socio-economic factors while The National Literacy Trust (2018) claims that children who engage with literacy stand three times higher chances of being mentally well than those who don't. As such, we as schools have a responsibility to prioritise reading at every stage of our students' journey. (National Literacy Trust, n.d.)

Initiatives for Instilling Reading for Pleasure as a Habit:

1 Students in Years 7 and 8 have at least one Reading for Pleasure lesson every fortnight, through their English lessons, which take place in the library.

2 Specific time is dedicated to Reading for Pleasure for every tutor group in Years 7–10 during Extended Student Guidance Time.

3 Tutor groups in Years 7–10 are provided with bespoke suggested reading lists, from which tutors can choose to read to their tutor groups during the course of the year.

4 Our Patron of Reading works closely with the school to provide support and opportunities for various groups of students.

5 Our Patron of Writing runs writing workshops with students, whose work is then shared with the rest of the school through a variety of media.

6 Our Library Manager organises a range of exciting author visits to the school throughout the year.

7 Both our Library Manager and English Department run book-related visits throughout the year.

8 Students are rewarded for reading with House Points: the tutor group and individual who read the most throughout the course of the school year receive a book-related prize.

However we decide to avail the opportunities that tutor time presents, it is indisputable that tutors offer invaluable stability and comfort to students each day. Marland and Rogers sum it up perfectly: "A form tutor is a teacher whose subject is the pupil herself" (Marland and Rogers, 2004). But what does this support mean to our students, and what do they really value about tutor time? My best advice is to have a strategy for collating feedback and to ask the people who matter most – our students.

Possible questions to ask students

● What do you enjoy most about tutor time at the school?

● What attributes do you most value in your tutor?

● How do the activities offered help your mornings?

● Are there any aspects of tutor time you don't enjoy? How would you like to see these change?

● What else would you like to see in tutor time?

● Would physical exercise or mindfulness help you?

● What is the significance of tutor time in your day?

● If you could plan a tutor time activity, what would it look like?

A second note

The power of our voices

The limits of my language are the limits of my world.
Ludwig Wittgenstein

This second note is the result of a conversation with my wonderfully clever colleague, Stella Vassiliou, who is the kind of teacher every parent wishes their child to be taught by. While this occasionally makes the rest of us a little jealous, we are usually far more preoccupied with being in awe of her! Stella and I see a natural and powerful synergy between her wider school remit, oracy, and mine, Ethos. I spent a glorious afternoon talking to her about this connection and her vision for our young leaders when it comes to oracy. She started out by explaining to me with absolute conviction that oracy is a 'right' that all students should be entitled to, at every stage of their school lives. She believes that all young people should have access to learning how to speak well and that their lives would be 'seriously impoverished' without this ability.

Given our 'moral imperative' to build student experience and confidence, it also falls on us to equip students to use their voices to be erudite, accurate, and fluent. It is not enough to have the tools to speak, Stella explained, but the real aim is to speak effectively. This is when we are truly heard and valued.

On their website, Voice 21 describe the significance of oracy as follows

In school, oracy is a powerful tool for learning; by teaching students to become more effective speakers and listeners we empower them to better understand themselves, each other and the world around them. It is also a route to social mobility, empowering all students, not just some, to find their voice to succeed in school and life.

(voice21.org, 2022)

Stella's work at the Trust is inspired very much by this aim and it is not difficult to see how crucial the oracy project is to any work we do to build young leadership

DOI: 10.4324/9781003275985-14

skills. As part of the oracy project, 'Face2Face' sessions are an integral part of tutor time, and students in every year group have a chance to experience debating, discussion, and talking to a purpose. Students need to be able to talk confidently and articulately about the things that really matter to them and the ability to do so generates more interest and engagement with the world around them. Even when students choose not to actively partake in discussions, they are being exposed to the world of conversation and to a rich assortment of vocabulary that they will begin to absorb. In addition, we employ our three non-negotiables through every lesson, to bolster students' confidence with using their voices effectively:

- *no opt out*

- *clear, audible classroom voice*

- *detailed verbal responses*

Over the years, these have become part of our teaching and learning fabric and a baseline expectation, for both students and staff.

Stella spoke to me about how she finds it 'crushing' when a student tells her that 'nothing matters' to them; this, she argues, is where oracy can make a profound difference. There is not much young people can do with their curiosity, fascination, or outrage at the world around them if they don't also have the tools to express these feelings accurately. In the state school sector, there seems to be less of an expectation for all students to speak well – not necessarily from schools themselves, but from society at large. The assumption that students in the independent sector will be better equipped with oracy skills can become a self-fulfilling prophecy and it is up to us to address this imbalance and 'level the playing field'.

Stella also talked passionately about the link between oracy and well-being, explaining that often students don't explain the specifics of what they find challenging because they just don't have the vocabulary to do this. Seen this way, it is 'cruel' to deny them the opportunity to share, explore, and achieve as they journey through school; language becomes a blunt instrument rather than a beautifully crafted one. One of the things that particularly struck me in my conversation with Stella was her absolute determination that students can be articulate in whatever accent they have and use. As a society that remains painfully classist, this disclaimer is an important one to make. When it comes to individual idiolects and sociolects, the oracy strategy does not aim to erase these. Instead, there is an appropriateness of language and the ability to switch code as in when we need to, which needs to be privileged. The aim is not to threaten the uniqueness of our young people but rather to celebrate it while simultaneously equipping them with the skills they need to succeed in any aspect of life.

This toolkit of oracy superpowers has never been more important than currently, where post lockdown, we are noticing the impact of isolated learning in our classrooms. Teachers all over the country and indeed all over the world have talked about the negative effects of the lockdown on student confidence and classroom talk. As we bolster the knowledge, leadership skills and values of our young people, we will do well to keep investing in their oracy skills and ultimately in the power of their voices (Figure 14.1).

Here is Stella's training for young speakers, distilled for the purpose of this book:

Miss Vassiliou, January 2023

Public Speaking Training for Student Leaders
Key Reminders

The Four Strands of Oracy*	• Physical • Linguistic • Cognitive • Social and emotional
Posture	• 'Own' the space • Ground yourself in your stance and avoid crossing your legs • Use open body language and remember that your gestures must match what you say, to be convincing
Connect with your audience	• Make eye contact (or pretend to!) • Consider where to stand in relation to your slides, if you have them
After your presentation	• Stand and wait for applause • Avoid rushing away
Use slides effectively	• Remember that the slides are there to support, not to replace, what you say • No more than 7 words per line; no more than 7 lines • Use images to replace words, where possible
Presenting well	• Find the magic point between engaging with the audience and looking at your slides • Find the magic point between preparation/practice and spontaneity
Preparing well	• Preparing slides is not enough: you must rehearse • Know your slides • Consider having a print-out, perhaps with notes, but not too many
Managing nerves	• Remember that all presenters get nervous • Prepare well and practise • Speak more slowly than you think you need to • Drink water • Look for friendly faces in the audience and try to enjoy it!

*The Four Strands of Oracy is a term used by Professor Neil Mercer in the Oracy Cambridge and Voice 21 'Oracy Framework'

Figure 14.1 Public Speaking Training for Student Leaders document.

Thought for the term entries

A selection

As promised earlier, here is a selection of entries for our thought for the term. These entries are shared with students, staff, and parents weekly, and staff and student leaders contribute on a rota basis. They drop into inboxes every Friday, to end the week feeling tired but inspired! Enjoy!

Thought for the term: commitment

For all of us involved in education, September is a time of new beginnings. Despite many years in teaching, I never fail to have butterflies on the first day back: a heady mix of anticipation and excitement for the year ahead, which lies waiting full of promise. With each school year come new resolutions and ambitious hopes. The real challenge, as we know, lies in staying the course in the weeks that follow. As the new term gets underway, those resolutions can be easily forgotten. Sticking to our goals and the promises we make ourselves takes real commitment. Commitment to stay the course and not allow the urgent to crowd out the important but also commitment to believe in ourselves and stay true to the ambition we have for the year ahead. After 18 months of Covid-19 disruption, this start of term feels especially new and exciting. As we begin the process of returning to a new normality, I want to commit to being optimistic and resolute in the months ahead. Walt Whitman said, "Keep your face always toward the sunshine and shadows will fall behind you." Remaining hopeful even when there are shadows takes commitment and strength and I know without doubt that our school community has that in abundance. It's going to be a fantastic year.

Georgina Littler, Headteacher, Didcot Girls' School

Thought for the term: commitment

Of the three touchstone values that we champion at St Birinus School, care, courtesy, and commitment, it is commitment that I feel that I have focused on so explicitly

DOI: 10.4324/9781003275985-15

over these first few days as our community has returned. With all our hopes and optimism for the year ahead, it is easy to say that to achieve in learning, and life, simply requires a capacity and desire to work hard, but commitment is more than just graft and grind. When you commit and when you commit fully, your ambition will demand sustained determination, concentration, and resilience. This commitment requires a very conscious decision and, at points, a leap of faith. But what better time to make that leap than now? The start of the new academic year, rich in energy and excitement, allows us all to reboot and refocus on what matters most in terms of achievement and accomplishment. There may be fleeting moments of hesitation, as within wholehearted commitment there lies the potential for failure but the beauty of that is that the bumps in the road are inextricably linked to our eventual success and actualising our potential.

Mr W Manning, Headteacher, St Birinus School

Thought for the term: commitment

With each start to a new school year, I begin a whole host of commitments to different things: learning more, reading more, writing more, being more efficient, more organised, more productive; it's a long list of 'mores' that I want to keep improving on each year. This year, I am adding something new to the list – my commitment to look after my well-being and seeking joy wherever possible. The context to this is rather self-evident, of course, and after the strangeness of the past 18 months or so I am convinced that we must seek joy in the little things, wherever and whenever possible. While this sounds wonderful, you might be wondering how I will go about making this change and I have a few thoughts for you: (1) Be mindful: try to stay in the present moment a few times every day. I do this very consciously now and it's helpful especially if you are feeling overwhelmed with lots to do. It's important to anchor yourself in the 'now' and leave the past and the future alone for a few moments to remind yourself how perfectly peaceful and wonderful the present moment is. It works! (2) Befriend nature: the delightful thing about nature is that it is constant and reliable, ready for you to enjoy whenever you wish. Whether it's a long walk along a familiar route, a more adventurous hike somewhere new, or just sitting in the outdoors soaking the autumnal sunshine, nature has the power to refresh us and fill us with renewed hope. (3) Lose yourself in a book: I know as schools we are meant to encourage you to read, but I am sure many of you will recognise the amazing ability of a book to transport us into marvellous new worlds and there is certainly good reason why they are called "uniquely portable magic". Reading new books and revisiting old favourites are highly recommended as ways to add more joy to our lives anytime we like. (4) Do a little more of what you love: for me, this is baking at home, with Classic FM playing in the background, and nothing to rush me – you will no doubt have your own ways to indulge your favourite hobbies. It's important to be productive, but there is a time to slow down and luxuriate in the activities we find joyous. (5) Keep connected: you don't even have to be an expert in well-being to know this but staying connected with each other, showing and seeking empathy, and finding time to relax with the people we love is incredibly powerful. Often, a small gesture of kindness on our part can make a big difference to someone else's day. That is a beautiful thing to know, isn't it? So, there we are: that is my commitment to myself this year and if I have helped to recognise the importance of looking after yourself in some small way too, even better!

Dr Khan, Director of Ethos, Ridgeway Education Trust

Thought for the term: commitment

Commitment – what does it mean to me? The Oxford Languages' definition of commitment is a pledge or bond to a certain course or policy. To be dedicated. I know that for me, commitment hasn't always come easily. It's a daily struggle to gain the motivation to uphold your word, whether that be to those close to you, your work, or even to yourself. In my experience, it is quite often the last one that's the hardest. Being committed to our family and friends is an act of love through dedication. It's keeping our promises and not letting people down. But it's also more than that. It's staying by the ones we love no matter what. Throughout lockdown, I saw many of my friends suffering through quarantine, struggling with the presence of mental illness, but we stuck together. We made time to check up on each other, making sure everyone was looking after themselves. It became part of the daily routine to make sure that everyone was eating and drinking properly. Because cliché as it is, the ultimate sign of friendship and love is to stay committed to each other through wind, rain, and fire. Regardless of what happens, we know that we have each other. Commitment to work is something that I know everyone has struggled with – I certainly have, especially as pressure builds. I find myself procrastinating and sometimes, on cold, dark mornings, I must dig deep for the motivation to get out of bed and get prepared for my day. I am someone who personally struggles to lead myself, to motivate myself, but with the prospect of exams closing in and the fantastic opportunities offered at school – I am switched on and working hard for the grades I want – by committing. People often say that effort is the key to success. They're right but it's not a one-off occurrence. You have to consistently commit. If you commit to your work, study when you need to, and uphold a good work/life balance, then you'll go far in life and succeed at whatever job you come to do. On top of that, the commitment will lead to achievements, and achievements bring happiness. Finally, I'd like to talk about perhaps the most important and most challenging aspect of commitment to yourself. This includes looking after yourself on a basic level such as drinking, eating, and sleeping enough as well as keeping your promises to yourself. Think back to New Year – How many of you committed to your resolutions? I'm sure many of you are very much enjoying your daily 5k runs or speaking in those newly learnt languages. Even if you fell just short of the goal, you were dedicated and you worked towards those intentions, and for that, you should be proud. Thank you for reading, Stay committed!

Asher Wong, Associate Head Boy (2021–2022),
St Birinus School

Thought for the term: creativity

To my knowledge, or indeed to my face, I have never been described as creative and when I personally reflect on the essence of creativity, I recognise that my immediate and instinctive definition is both narrow and un-encompassing. My mind leaps to an artistic process, to imagination, self-expression, and freedom in what some might perceive as an innate, unpredictable, and perhaps unteachable skill. Far from it. In a time recently when as individuals, families, and organisations, we have had to problem solve, adapt, and find alternatives, creativity, innovation, and the formation of valuable new ideas have been at an absolute premium. Genuine creativity combines instinct, personal motivation, and the courage of a venturesome and brave personality. It thrives in the right environment, one that is inclusive, open to self-expression, and the desire and poise to see things differently. As Eric Fromm, the famous 20th-century social psychologist, once said, "Creativity requires the courage to let go of certainty". To allow creativity to flourish, we often have to let go of what is, to us, safe and assured. We have to let go of fear and our preconceptions – what we already know. The real joy of creativity comes from both pushing for something new and the realisation that, unlike many things in life, the more you use, the more you have.

Mr W Manning, Headteacher, St Birinus School

Thought for the term: creativity

One of my favourite places when I was at school was the corridor of art classrooms; each one a riot of colour and texture, getting smaller and smaller as you made your way into the building. On the walls were crowded images of the exquisitely realistic and the alarmingly unfamiliar: human bodies, natural forms, and everyday objects competing for attention. At the centre was a small projector room, with blackened walls and a collection of small rickety chairs pointing at a screen. We would gather round, plunged into darkness before the projector flickered into action and sit entranced by our teacher's descriptions of bold abstracts and fluid lines. We were surrounded by creativity. But when it came to it, brush poised above the paper, the instruction to 'be creative' could often feel like a roadblock. The pressure to produce something worthy felt enormous, but the reality is that creativity is a process not a destination. It comes in many forms and looks different to different people. Creativity is taking the time to share your perspective on the world. It is finding the beauty in the everyday and finding ways to represent information and share your views. It is being responsive and resourceful: changing your mind, adapting your approach, and inspiring others to come with you. Whatever it is that you create, be proud of the perspective you have shared.

Mrs F Ashton, Assistant Head, Teaching & Learning,
RET Associate Director of Education

Thought for the term: care

Care has many definitions: showing personal interest or care, paying attention to detail, looking after something, providing protection, or regarding something highly. To me, caring means opening your heart to something you feel strongly about and not hiding away from the range of feelings that come with that. And most importantly, care links to the people that you love and trust the most. Perhaps when it's broken down like that, the idea of care can seem daunting, but in reality, it is woven intrinsically into the human experience and is what makes life so beautiful. In fact, having people who look out for you and looking out for others is one of the most important factors in life. Luckily, there's an exceptional amount of care shown within our school community on a daily basis; be that students offering each other help with academics while simultaneously looking out for their classmate's well-being or teachers planning an activity in their lessons specifically because they know their class will love it. Care is all around us, and I think it is one of the things that makes Didcot Girls' School such a successful and thriving teaching and learning environment. Recently, I have been involved in the RET's incredibly successful production of We Will Rock You. After (rather emotionally) reflecting on it over these last few days, it just might be the most prolific example of what it means to care deeply and how much you can achieve when you're committed to something that I've seen throughout my time at DGS. It was a privilege to be part of. Our fantastic cast spent almost 100 hours in rehearsals since late-September and the staff involved easily exceeded that amount of effort with all the tireless hard work they put in behind the scenes – we wouldn't have had a show without them! The time and energy we put into the project was no mean feat and putting it simply, if we didn't love it, we wouldn't have done it. Theatre is something I care profoundly about, and I truly have never cherished a group of people or experience more than this. It exemplified just how much can be achieved when people work together towards a goal, and we did it with a bang. I tell you this to remind you that without caring about something, there is little point in doing it. Without caring, it is impossible to find the motivation to wind-up prosperous in the end. And with care comes the possibility of tremendous achievement. Care is fundamental to leading a fulfilling life, because without care what is passion, commitment, or joy?

Sydnie Dougan, House Captain of Wilson House

Thought for the term: diversity

So, what do we mean by diversity and why is it important? Diversity can be defined as the condition or fact of being different or varied. Over recent years, it has taken on a more specific meaning relating to the characteristics of a group of people. When people write and speak about diversity in the media, they are most often talking about difference in terms of the characteristics protected in the Equality Act of 2010: race, religion, sex, sexuality, gender reassignment, pregnancy, disability, marriage, and age, but we could go further and include class or financial situation, education, or any other aspect of a person's identity. We can all describe our identity through a diversity lens but one person on their own cannot be diverse – we need a group. As Bryony Landsbert wrote earlier this term, our instinct as humans is often to make connections with people who are most like us and we can end up in a little bubble of people who look like us, think like us, and have the same experiences as us. I'm still close friends with people I met at university who happened to live on the same staircase as me; unsurprisingly, a lot of my friends are teachers. Having obvious things in common is often a way into a conversation or the beginning of a relationship; it can feel safe and comfortable to be with others who are similar to us. But if we only stick to what we know, we are all missing out, and some of us will be missing out more than others, if we are excluded from groups or opportunities because of our gender or race or disability or other aspect of our identity. So that's why is it important to think about and celebrate and increase the diversity of our Trust community and our schools. Everyone is entitled to a safe place to learn. Everyone should experience a curriculum that reflects their own experiences and teaches them about the wider world. Everyone is entitled to opportunities to develop and lead. Everyone has an experience and story to share that enriches our community. Everyone belongs here.

Mrs B Bowers, Deputy Headteacher, St Birinus School

Thought for the term: appreciating education

"..Let us pick up our books and our pens, they are the most powerful weapons. One child, one teacher, one book and one pen can change the world."

Malala Yousafzai

Some 19 years ago, I worked for some time teaching in an international school in Manila, in the Philippines. The Philippines are incredibly beautiful islands where the landscape is breath-taking and white sand beaches and azure blue seas abound. I love to scuba dive and I absolutely love the sea so I felt very fortunate to work there and be able to spend my weekends diving with manta rays and sharks. An amazing experience.

The school I worked in was located in a very wealthy district of Manila. The weather was generally very warm and we had nice air-conditioned classrooms and a swimming pool. We had great computer facilities and opportunities to go on school trips to Hong Kong, Malaysia, and Indonesia. We only played sport with other international schools; my friends were international teachers so I didn't initially have much of an idea of what life might be like for other people in the local area who may be less fortunate.

My son was very little when I worked in Manila and he had a childminder when we were at work, her name was Margie and we are still good friends. Margie talked to me about her children and their school experience. She explained that the local school, just a few miles from my school, had to operate in shifts as there were too many students to all attend at once. Quite a few students walked a long way to get to school as they didn't have the financial means to get there by bus or car. That same year, I had the opportunity to volunteer at the local school after my school day finished as the second shift of the day at that school ran until 7 pm. It was an incredible experience. The classrooms were very hot, with no luxuries like air conditioning or computer facilities; they were also very busy with 60–70 children crammed onto long benches in each room and the teacher explaining using chalk and a blackboard. More powerfully, the classrooms were overflowing with joy and a willingness to learn in order to have choices for a better future, hence being prepared to come to school in shifts and walk a very long way. The children were, without exception, full of enthusiasm to learn English with me, to sing songs and chant new vocabulary, even though we didn't have textbooks or computers or many resources. They were friendly, warm, respectful, and I loved every minute of my time there, just as I loved my classes at the international school where I worked and just as I get tremendous joy from my role as a headteacher. The differences in facilities may have been stark but the similarities in terms of working with a group of enthusiastic young people, keen to learn and grow, really were much greater.

At a time where the world does not always feel full of positive news, I often think back to those days in Manila and reflect on how much I learnt about the power of education to transform lives and the absolute privilege that learning brings us to enable us to have choices and opportunity. I never thought one school was better than the other, but I did feel a profound sense of injustice at the privilege my classes had compared to the working conditions at the local school where I volunteered. It's so easy to forget what we have. It isn't necessarily better but we are fortunate to have freedom and the opportunity to learn, simply at our fingertips. Education truly is the most powerful weapon of all.

Georgina Littler, Headteacher, Didcot Girls' School

Bibliography

African Children's Fund. (n.d.). *Home.* [online] Available at: https://www.africanchildrens-fund.org/.

Andrew Bryant and Ana Lucia Kazan (2012). *Self-leadership: how to become a more successful, efficient, and effective leader from the inside out.* New York: Mcgraw Hill Professional.

Barrett, R. (2013). *Building a values-driven organization a whole system approach to cultural transformation.* London: Routledge.

Brown, B. (2012). *Daring greatly: how the courage to be vulnerable transforms the way we live, love, parent, and Lead.* New York: Gotham Books.

Bubb, S. (n.d.). *Outward-facing schools: the Sinnott Fellowship.* [online] Available at: https://assets.publishing.service.gov.uk/government/uploads/system/uploads/attach-ment_data/file/490831/DFE-RR139.pdf [Accessed 5 Feb. 2023].

Cain, S. (2013). *Quiet: the power of introverts in a world that can't stop talking.* London: Penguin Books.

Clinton, C. (2018). *She persisted.* New York: Philomel Books.

Cordova, Esther Pia and Adiputri, Maima Widya (2017). *I can't do that, yet: growth mindset.* North Charleston, SC: Createspace Independent Publishing Platform.

Department for Education (2019). *Department for education.* [online] Available at: https://www.gov.uk/government/organisations/department-for-education [Accessed 6 Feb. 2023].

Dweck, C.S. (2017). *Mindset: changing the way you think to fulfil your potential.* London: Robinson.

Handscombe, J. (2021). *A school built on ethos.* White Plains, NY: Crown House Publishing Ltd.

Johnston, H. (2020). *What role does the House system play in a modern school?* [online] Available at: http://whs-blogs.co.uk/teaching/role-house-system-play-modern-school/ [Accessed 5 Feb. 2023].

Kahnweiler, J.B. and Conant, D.R. (2018). *The introverted leader: building on your quiet strength.* Oakland, CA: Berrett-Koehler Publishers, Inc.

Khan, G. (n.d.). *Day-to-day approaches to the growth mindset.* [online] Available at: https://seced.mydigitalpublication.co.uk/articles/day-to-day-approaches-to-the-growth-mindset.

Lowrie, L. (2019). *Vulnerability in the classroom.* [online] Available at: https://www.facultyfocus.com/articles/teaching-and-learning/vulnerability-in-the-classroom/.

Marland, M. and Rogers, R. (2004). *How to be a successful form tutor.* London: Continuum.

Milbrey Wallin Mclaughlin (2018). *You can't be what you can't see: the power of opportunity to change young lives*. Cambridge, MA: Harvard Education Press.

Moore, K. (2017). *Two days with Warren Buffett: three lessons from an introverted leader in action. Forbes*. [online] Available at: https://www.forbes.com/sites/karlmoore/2017/05/05/spending-2-days-with-warren-buffett-3-lessons-from-an-introverted-leader-in-action/?sh=481c1466cfe5.

National Literacy Trust. (n.d.). *National Literacy Trust | UK Literacy Charity*. [online] Available at: https://literacytrust.org.uk/?gclid=CjwKCAiAxP2eBhBiEiwA5puhNTUX9AH-GGTJthS8T329j9llzkiJZ2XDd8lr8-73qrgXCtbcUjsUOvxoCBYsQAvD_BwE [Accessed 6 Feb. 2023].

Ng, B. (2018). The neuroscience of growth mindset and intrinsic motivation. *Brain Sciences*, [online] 8(2), p.20. https://doi.org/10.3390/brainsci8020020.

Outen, S. (2018). *Dare to Do*. Boston, MA: Nicholas Brealey.

Outen, S. (n.d.). *Sarah Outen | London2London: via the World*. [online] *London2London*. Available at: http://www.sarahouten.com/.

Picardo, J. (2012). *Why students need a global awareness and understanding of other cultures. The Guardian*. [online] Available at: https://www.theguardian.com/teacher-network/2012/sep/25/students-global-awareness-other-cultures [Accessed 5 Feb. 2023].

Quigley, A. (2020). *Closing the reading gap*. New York: Routledge.

Shaw, C. (n.d.). *5 ways to create a great global school partnership*. TES.

Smith, J. (2022). *Why has nobody told me this before?* New York: Harperone.

Strauss, N. (2007). *The game*. Edinburgh: Canongate Books.

Suni, Eric (2000). *National sleep foundation*. [online] Available at: https://www.sleepfoundation.org/ [Accessed 6 Feb. 2023].

Sydney, A., Deuter, M., Bradbery, J. and Turnbull, J. (2015). *Oxford advanced learner's dictionary of current English*. Oxford: Oxford University Press.

Syed, M. (2010). *Bounce: Mozart, Federer, Picasso, Tiger, and the science of success*. New York: Harper.

Syed, M. (2015). *Black box thinking*. New York: Penguin Publishing Group.

Syed, M. (2022). Rebel ideas: the power of diverse thinking. New York: Flatiron Books.

voice21.org. (2022). *Become a voice 21 oracy school - Voice 21*. [online] Available at: https://voice21.org/work-with-us/?gclid=CjwKCAiAxP2eBhBiEiwA5puhNdZHuzGQ33U7lX-rTg0O3ksJmdtH4huE_Ij8KPeMAJZFsEeI5n7LEVBoCb9oQAvD_BwE [Accessed 6 Feb. 2023].

Wilson, T., Wood, L. and Perfect, E. (2017). *The cow tripped over the moon*. Glen Huntly, VIC: Story Box Library.

www.didcotgirls.oxon.sch.uk. (n.d.). *Welcome to Didcot Girls' School*. [online] Available at: https://www.didcotgirls.oxon.sch.uk/ [Accessed 6 Feb. 2023].

www.didcotsixthform.co.uk. (n.d.). *Welcome to Didcot Sixth Form - Didcot Sixth Form*. [online] Available at: https://www.didcotsixthform.co.uk/ [Accessed 6 Feb. 2023].

www.ridgewayeducationtrust.co.uk. (n.d.). *Welcome to Ridgeway Education Trust*. [online] Available at: https://www.ridgewayeducationtrust.co.uk/ [Accessed 5 Feb. 2023].

Index

Note: *Italic* page numbers refer to figures.

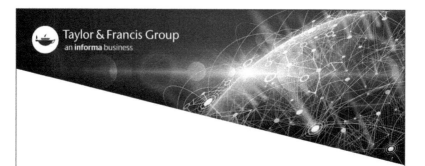